P9-CCP-174

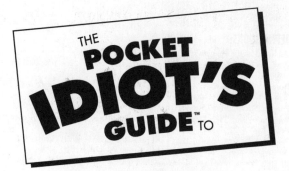

THE POCKET IDIOT'S GUIDE TO

German Phrases

by Angelika Körner and Susan Shelly

ALPHA

A member of Penguin Group (USA) Inc.

ALPHA BOOKS

Published by the Penguin Group

Penguin Group (USA) Inc., 375 Hudson Street, New York, New York 10014, U.S.A.

Penguin Group (Canada), 10 Alcorn Avenue, Toronto, Ontario, Canada M4V 3B2 (a division of Pearson Penguin Canada Inc.)

Penguin Books Ltd, 80 Strand, London WC2R 0RL, England

Penguin Ireland, 25 St Stephen's Green, Dublin 2, Ireland (a division of Penguin Books Ltd)

Penguin Group (Australia), 250 Camberwell Road, Camberwell, Victoria 3124, Australia (a division of Pearson Australia Group Pty Ltd)

Penguin Books India Pvt Ltd, 11 Community Centre, Panchsheel Park, New Delhi—110 017, India

Penguin Group (NZ), cnr Airborne and Rosedale Roads, Albany, Auckland 1310, New Zealand (a division of Pearson New Zealand Ltd)

Penguin Books (South Africa) (Pty) Ltd, 24 Sturdee Avenue, Rosebank, Johannesburg 2196, South Africa

Penguin Books Ltd, Registered Offices: 80 Strand, London WC2R 0RL, England

International Standard Book Number: 1-59257-366-5
Library of Congress Catalog Card Number: 2005920507

12   11   10   8   7

Interpretation of the printing code: The rightmost number of the first series of numbers is the year of the book's printing; the rightmost number of the second series of numbers is the number of the book's printing. For example, a printing code of 05-1 shows that the first printing occurred in 2005.

Printed in the United States of America

Note: This publication contains the opinions and ideas of its authors. It is intended to provide helpful and informative material on the subject matter covered. It is sold with the understanding that the authors and publisher are not engaged in rendering professional services in the book. If the reader requires personal assistance or advice, a competent professional should be consulted.

The authors and publisher specifically disclaim any responsibility for any liability, loss, or risk, personal or otherwise, which is incurred as a consequence, directly or indirectly, of the use and application of any of the contents of this book.

Most Alpha books are available at special quantity discounts for bulk purchases for sales promotions, premiums, fund-raising, or educational use. Special books, or book excerpts, can also be created to fit specific needs.

For details, write: Special Markets, Alpha Books, 375 Hudson Street, New York, NY 10014.

To my grandfather, Theo Körner.

Contents

Introduction

So you've decided you want to get familiar with the German language, or maybe brush up on some knowledge you might have forgotten. As you learn or relearn the language, know that you're in good company. More than 100 million people worldwide speak German, making it one of the most commonly used languages.

Tackling a new language can be a little scary, but it also can be exciting and fun. Sure, it's challenging to push yourself to learn something new, but the results are sure to be worthwhile.

If you're worried that learning German phrases might be too much of a chore, you can relax. German and English are first cousins in the language world, sharing many words that are identical or very similar. Although German is a foreign language, you'll find that it's really not all that foreign.

This book teaches you a great deal of German that will help you navigate your way through a German-speaking country and converse with German-speaking people. Although you won't be exactly an expert in the language when you finish this book, you should feel confident enough to try out your new vocabulary as needed, trusting that people will understand what you're saying.

Finding time to study and practice German phrases will require a bit of a commitment on your part, but this book is set up in a way that you can pick and choose the parts of the language that are most applicable to you. If you're going to be visiting Germany, for instance, before your trip you can read the chapter containing the phrases you'll need on your way there. Then, when you're on the plane, you can study the chapter that will help you check into your hotel.

So settle back and begin your journey toward learning some phrases in a new language. We think you'll enjoy the trip.

Extras

Included in the chapters of this book are three kinds of sidebars, all intended to provide information you'll find useful and valuable. Here's what to look for:

Watch It! _____

These boxes warn of potential language, social, and cultural faux pas.

What's This? _____

Check these boxes for grammar tidbits and explanations of terminology with which you might not be familiar.

While We're at It _____

These boxes provide tips, offbeat information, and more to give you insights into the German language and culture.

Acknowledgments

The authors would like to thank the many people who provided time, information, and resources for this book. Special thanks to our editors at Alpha Books, whose keen eyes and expertise always turn out a better product than the one that was submitted. And thanks also go to Gene Brissie of James Peter Associates as well.

Thank you and much love to our families, and special thanks to Stephanie Rieffanaugh.

Special Thanks to the Technical Reviewer

The Pocket Idiot's Guide to German Phrases was reviewed by an expert who double-checked the accuracy of what you'll learn here, to help us ensure that this book gives you the phrases you need to know about to get around in a German-speaking country. Special thanks are extended to Jeff Poth.

Jeff Poth is a graduate of Rutgers College, New Brunswick, New Jersey, with a degree in German, economics, and art history. He graduated as a member of the German Honor Society and has studied at the University of Constance, Germany. He currently heads Poth Audio, designing and manufacturing audio components, in addition to a number of other occupations.

Trademarks

So You Want to Learn to Speak German

In This Chapter

- Understanding the similarities between German and English
- Keeping your cool while learning the language
- Language learning tips
- Pronouncing German words and phrases

Attempting to learn a new language can be a daunting task, there's no question about it. As our world gets smaller, however, having a handle on different cultures and languages becomes increasingly important.

Although German might look and sound completely foreign to you—no pun intended—you'll be surprised at the similarities found between German and English. For now, try not to think about the differences between the two languages, and let's take a look at how they're really not all that far apart.

The Similarities Between German and English

English is a Germanic language, along with other languages such as Dutch and Yiddish. German and English are first cousins, which accounts for the great similarity of many words.

Winter, Finger, and *Land*—words you recognize as English words—are also German words.

Other German words such as *Mutter, Brot,* and *Feuer* are not as obvious to translate, but when you know they mean "mother," "bread," and "fire," they become easy to remember.

In addition, German and English have borrowed many words from other languages, particularly from Greek and Latin. Such words include *Telefon, Butter, aktiv, studieren,* and *Theater.*

Languages intertwine as new words pop up. As a result, German recently has adopted many English words, such as *software, Internet,* and *airbag.* Words used frequently in American advertising, such as *fresh, cool,* and *happy,* also have been added to the German language, along with pop-culture terms such as *Hard Rock, Filmstars,* and *Popmusik.*

All this sharing and borrowing adds up, and, at last count, more than 40 percent of all German words have English *cognates.*

What's This?

Two related words in different languages are called **cognates**. Some English-German cognates are almost identical in spelling and meaning, whereas others are just similar.

Things aren't always as they appear, however, so don't assume that all words that seem to be cognates really are. Beware of a group of words called "false cognates." They seem like cognates, but they have quite different meanings. A few examples are listed in Table 1.1.

Table 1.1   False Cognate Examples

German	English	Pronunciation
das Gift	the poison	*dahs gift*
das Handy	the cell phone	*dahs handy*
der Mist	the manure	*dair mist*
nein	no	*nine*
der Notfall	the emergency	*dair noht-fahl*
rot	red	*roht*
war	was	*vahr*
was	what	*vahs*
wer	who	*vair*
wo	where	*voh*

The underlined text in the Pronunciation column is the syllable to stress when pronouncing the word. See the "Pronouncing Just About Anything in German" section, later in this chapter, for more on pronunciation.

False cognates are the exception to the rule, though. In most cases, what looks to be a cognate really is a cognate.

Staying Cool and Calm

Learning a new language—any language—involves a fair number of mistakes. That's just a given. Do you remember when you were learning to drive a car? Or knit? Or play tennis? Or use a computer? Chances are you made some mistakes along the way; after all, by its very nature, learning includes mistakes.

Instead of getting uptight or embarrassed when you attempt to speak German to a native speaker, take a minute to think about the times you encountered someone whose native language wasn't English trying to speak it. Chances are you were patient and appreciative of the person's efforts to speak your language. And chances are the two of you managed some degree of understanding and communication.

And so it will be as you stumble through the early stages of speaking and understanding German. Be adventurous, stay calm, and enjoy the experience.

Tips for Learning a New Language (Especially German)

Learning a language is much like learning to play a musical instrument. You need to practice, and practice means repetition. When you think about it, that's how we all learned to talk as small children. We listened to the language being spoken all around us, and we eventually figured out what the words meant and how to say them.

Having someone around who speaks German while you're learning the language gives you a huge advantage. If you don't have a German speaker around, however, you can provide repetition for yourself:

- Use Post-It notes to identify items around your house with their German names.

- Write the German phrases for certain household activities on Post-It notes and place them in the area where the activity occurs. For instance, place a note with the phrase *Ich mache Kaffee* (I make coffee) by the coffee maker.

- Dedicate 10 minutes a day to reviewing phrases and vocabulary. Have a friend or relative quiz you.

- Check out language-learning resources and tutorials on the Internet. Many free sites offer vocabulary practice, and some even feature audio.

Sometimes students are advised to immerse themselves in the language they want to learn. Be sure to choose materials appropriate to your skill level if you go this route. For example, if you're a complete beginner, don't attempt to watch the latest news from Germany online or a German-language movie, or you'll just get frustrated. Rather, look for children's books and magazines, or videos and audiotapes geared to your skill level.

The best resources really are people. If you have the opportunity to spend some one-on-one time with a German speaker, he or she can adapt to your language level. That will give you a chance to try out what you've learned and to correct some of those inevitable mistakes. It will also give you invaluable opportunities for listening and understanding.

Pronouncing Just About Anything in German

If you're traveling, you'll come across many words—particularly names of people and places—you haven't learned in this book. Fortunately, it's not difficult to figure out the pronunciation of German words, because most German letters (with a few notable exceptions) sound the same as their English counterparts.

The pronunciation guide in Table 1.2 will help you pronounce the words and phrases listed throughout this book in a manner most German-speaking people will be able to understand.

Table 1.2   Pronunciation Guide

German Letter(s)	Approximate English Sound	Example
a	*ah*	father / sun
ä	*ay*	hair / met
au	*ow*	house, how
äu	*oy*	boy
ch	1. *H*	1. human (If you can't produce this sound, substitute *sh*.)
	2. *hk* (varies)	2. like Hebrew challah (If you can't produce this sound, substitute *k*.)
e	*eh*	may / met
ei	*ie*	mine, eye (Think of *Einstein*.)
eu	*oy*	boy
gn	*g-n*	(Pronounce both letters separately.)
i	*ih*	inn, sit
ie	*ee*	see (Think of wiener.)
j	*y*	yes
kn	*k-n*	(Pronounce both letters separately.)
o	*oh*	boat
ö	*u(r)*	curl
ps	*p-s*	(Pronounce both letters separately.)
qu	*k-v*	(Instead of English *k-w*) Qualität; quality
s	1. *s*	1. sit
	2. *z* (varies)	2. rose

continues

Table 1.2 Pronunciation Guide (continued)

German Letter(s)	Approximate English Sound	Example
ß	*s*	sit
sch	*sh*	short
sp	*sh-p*	(Instead of English *s-p*) Spiel; match
st	*sh-t*	(Instead of English *s-t*) Straße; street
th	*t*	ten
u	*oo*	pool / bush
ü	*ew*	(This sound has no English equivalent.) über; over
v	*f*	four
w	*v*	very
z	*ts*	cats

Two exceptions to the German-letters-sounding-like-English-letters rule are *l* and *r*. To really learn these sounds, you need to listen closely to a native German speaker. (You'll still be understood if you maintain your English *l* and *r* sounds though.)

While We're at It

If your goal is near-native pronunciation, ask native speakers to sound out words for you. Most people, when asked nicely, will gladly help you. Of course, you can listen to CDs or tapes to help you practice different sounds as well.

You've probably noticed that some German vowels, such as ä, ö, and ü, have two dots over them. The two dots are called an *Umlaut* (*oom-lowt*), and the umlaut changes the vowel's sound.

The sound of the ä is similar to English *hair* or *let*, but ü and ö do not have English equivalents. You can practice ü by saying *iii* (as in *see*). Hold that sound while you close your lips round, so they are in the form of the sound *oo*. Similarly, try to pronounce German *e* (as in *may*) while rounding your lips.

If the *a*, *o*, and *u* vowel sounds seem too complicated, just ignore the umlaut and pronounce them as you normally would. You won't sound like a native, but you can always work to improve your pronunciation when you're around people who use the real sounds.

What's This?

The letter ß, or *es-tset*, is peculiar to German. It is always pronounced as *s*, such as in *sit*.

By now you've probably figured out that your Volkswagen is really a *fohlks-vah-ghen* and Mozart is pronounced *moh-tsart*. Take a minute and try to pronounce the words in Table 1.3. Cover the Pronunciation column until you've made a good effort to pronounce the words on your own.

Table 1.3 German Pronunciations

German	Pronunciation
Darmstadt	*dahrm-shtat*
Einbahnstraße	*ien-bahn-shtrah-se*
Europa	*oy-roh-pah*
Freiburg	*frie-boorg*
Gotha	*goh-tah*
Jena	*yeh-nah*
Köln	*ku(r)ln*
Koblenz	*koh-blents*
München	*mewn-Hen*
Passau	*pah-sow*
Schwarzwald	*shvahrts-vahlt*
Speyer	*shpah-yer*
Viertel	*feer-tl*

WELCOME TO GERMANY **While We're at It**

As in English, German pronunciation tends to put the stress (the emphasis) on the first syllable of the word. The stressed syllables are underlined in the pronunciation guides throughout the book.

Chapter 2

Making Your Way to Germany

In This Chapter

- Phrases relating to airports and airplanes
- Mastering airplane lingo
- Locating your luggage in the airport
- Handling misunderstandings and language problems

You've purchased tickets and reserved your flight. You've made arrangements to have your plants watered and your mail held at the post office. Your bags are packed, your passport is in hand, and you're ready to head to the airport.

Embarking on any trip is an exciting proposition, especially one to a foreign country. It can also be a little daunting.

In this chapter, you learn the phrases you need to know to help get you to Germany—and through the airport after you're there. Be sure to pack this book in your carry-on bag or purse so you can study a bit on the plane!

At the Airport

Although you probably won't need to speak much German on your way to Germany, it doesn't hurt to be familiar with airport- and airplane-related terms and phrases. Study the terms in Table 2.1 to keep you in the know and help you communicate with airport personnel or other passengers.

Table 2.1 Airport and Airplane Phrases

English	German	Pronunciation
airline	die Fluglinie	dee _flook_-leen-yeh
airplane	das Flugzeug	dahs _flook_-tsoyk
airport	der Flughafen	dair _flook_-hah-fehn
arrival	die Ankunft	dee _ahn_-koonft
baggage claim	die Gepäckaus-gabe	dee geh-_payk_-ows-gah-beh
bathroom	die Toiletten / die WCs	dee toy-_letn_ / dee _veh_-tsehs
bus stop	die Bushalte-stelle	dee _boos_-hahl-teh-shtay-leh
car rental	der Mietwagen	dair _meet_-vah-gn
	der Leihwagen	dair _lie_-vah-gn
carry-on luggage	das Bordgepäck	dahs _board_-geh-pack
cart	der Wagen	dair _vah_-gn
counter	der Schalter	dair _shahl_-ter
departure	der Abflug	dair _ahb_-flook
delay	die Verspätung	dee fair-_shpay_-toonk

English	German	Pronunciation
elevator	der Aufzug / der Lift	*dair <u>owf</u>-tsook /* *dair lift*
entrance	der Eingang	*dair <u>ien</u>-gahng*
exit	der Ausgang	*dair <u>ows</u>-gahng*
final destination	der Ankunftsort	*dair <u>ahn</u>-koonfts-ohrt*
flight	der Flug	*dair flook*
gate	das Gate	*dahs gate*
information	die Information	*dee inn-for-mah-<u>tsyohn</u>*
	die Auskunft	*dee <u>ows</u>-koonft*
lost and found	das Fundbüro	*dahs <u>foond</u>-bew-roh*
to miss the flight	den Flug verpassen	*dayn flook <u>fair</u>-pahs-ahn*
money exchange	der Geldwechsel	*dair <u>gaylt</u>-vak-sl*
odd-size luggage	das Sperrgepäck	*dahs <u>shpayr</u>-geh-pack*
passport control	die Paßkontrolle	*dee <u>pahs</u>-kohn-troh-leh*
security check	die Sicherheitskontrolle	*dee <u>see</u>-Her-hiets-kohn-troh-leh*
stopover (in)	der Zwischenstop (in)	*dair <u>tsvee</u>-shehn-shtop (inn)*
suitcase	der Koffer	*dair <u>koh</u>-fr*
taxicab	das Taxi	*dahs <u>tahk</u>-see*
ticket	das Ticket	*dahs ticket*
train station	der Bahnhof	*dair <u>bahn</u>-hohf*
trip	die Reise	*dee rie-zeh*

On the Airplane

Personnel who work at all the major airlines that fly U.S. passengers to Germany, Austria, and Switzerland are able to speak English, so you won't need to sweat your German-speaking skills while you're in the air. However, you might need to be able to communicate with German-speaking passengers, so study Table 2.2 if you want to practice some in-flight phrases.

What's This?

If you've noticed that the German words for the English *taxi*, *bathroom*, and *money exchange* are capitalized, that's because in German, all nouns are capitalized, no matter where they occur in the sentence. Adjectives of nationality, however, such as *German*, are not capitalized.

Table 2.2   Inside the Plane

English	German	Pronunciation
aisle	der Gang	*dair gahng*
to board the airplane	ins Flugzeug einsteigen	*eens floog-tsoyk ien-stie-gen*
crew	die Flugbegleiter (pl.)	*dee floog-beh-glie-ter*
emergency exit	der Notausgang	*dair noht-ows-gahng*
gate	das Gate	*dahs gate*
landing	die Landung	*dee lahn-doong*
life vest	die Schwimmweste	*dee shvihm-vehs-teh*
(non)smokers	(Nicht) Raucher	*(neeHt) raow-kher*
row	die Reihe	*dee rie-eh*
seat	der Sitz	*dair zits*
seatbelt	der Sicherheits- gurt	*dair see-Her-hiets- ghoort*
takeoff	der Abflug	*dair up-flook*

Locating Your Luggage

When you've reached the airport in Germany, you'll want to find your luggage so you can head to your destination. Use the phrases in Table 2.3 on your way to find your bags and sort out any problems you might encounter.

Table 2.3 At Baggage Claim

English	German	Pronunciation
Where is the counter?	Wo ist der Schalter?	*voh ist dair <u>shahl</u>-ter*
Where is the baggage claim?	Wo ist die Gepäckausgabe?	*voh ist dee geh-payk-ows-gah-beh*
Where is the oversize luggage?	Wo ist das Sperrgepäck?	*voh ist dahs <u>shpehr</u>-geh-payk*
I am missing (one) piece of luggage.	Mir fehlt ein Gepäckstück.	*meer faylt ien geh-<u>payk</u>-shtewk*
My luggage is damaged.	Mein Gepäck ist beschädigt.	*mien <u>geh-payk</u> ist beh-<u>shay</u>-deeHt*
Where is the flight to …?	Wo ist der Flug nach …?	*voo ist dair flook nahkh …*
It's over there.	Es ist dort.	*ehs ist dohrt*
It's in this direction.	Es ist hier entlang.	*ehs ist heer ehnt-<u>lahng</u>*
Go this way!	Gehen Sie hier entlang!	*<u>geh</u>-ehn zee heer ehnt-<u>lahng</u>*
Go up!	Gehen Sie hoch!	*<u>geh</u>-ehn zee hohkh*
Go down!	Gehen Sie runter!	*<u>geh</u>-ehn zee <u>roon</u>-ter*
Go back to …!	Gehen Sie zurück zu …!	*<u>geh</u>-hen zee tsoo-<u>rewk</u> tsoo …*
Go right!	Gehen Sie rechts!	*<u>geh</u>-hen zee rayHts*
Go left!	Gehen Sie links!	*<u>geh</u>-hen zee leenks*

Communicating in Difficult Situations

When a traveler is not fluent in the language of the country in which he or she is traveling, he or she is bound to hit some rough spots communicating. When you don't understand what someone is saying or are having difficulty making yourself understood, don't get frustrated or pretend you know more than you do. Simply use the phrases in Table 2.4 to inform the person you're speaking with that you're having some difficulty.

Table 2.4   When You Don't Understand

English	German	Pronunciation
Excuse me / Pardon	Entschuldigung	*ehn-tshool-dee-ghoong*
I don't understand.	Ich verstehe nicht.	*eeH fayr-shteh-eh neeHt*
Please repeat that.	Bitte wiederholen Sie das.	*bee-teh vee-der-hoh-len zee dahs*
Please speak more slowly.	Bitte sprechen Sie langsamer.	*bee-teh shpreh-Hen zee lahng-zah-mer*
I speak …	Ich spreche …	*eeH shpreh-Heh …*
English	Englisch	*ehng-lish*
German	Deutsch	*doytsh*
I don't speak (well) …	Ich spreche nicht (gut) …	*eeH shpreh-Heh neeHt (goot) …*
Do you speak …?	Sprechen Sie …?	*shpreh-Hen zee …*

Now that you've made it to Germany, you'll likely begin meeting some interesting people. In the next chapter, you learn how to ask others about themselves and share information about yourself.

Chapter 3

Getting to Know You

In This Chapter

- Breaking the ice
- Using question words
- Talking about yourself
- Introducing family members
- Understanding the informal "you"

During your visit to Germany, you'll no doubt meet many people. Naturally, you'll want to be able to tell them about yourself and find out more about them. In this chapter, you learn phrases that will make it easy for you to meet people and learn about their lives.

Greetings!

A nod and a smile go a long way toward letting someone know you are friendly and interested in getting better acquainted, but words and phrases will help you out a great deal as well. Table 3.1 lists some helpful introductory phrases and questions.

Table 3.1 Common Greetings and Questions

English	German	Pronunciation
Hello.	Hallo.	*hah-loh*
Good day.	Guten Tag.	*goo-ten tahk*
Good evening.	Guten Abend.	*goo-ten ah-bent*
Mr. / Sir	Herr	*behr*
Miss / Mrs.	Frau	*frow*
My name is …	Ich heiße …	*eeH hie-seh …*
What is your name?	Wie heißen Sie?	*vee hie-sen zee*
How are you?	Wie geht's?	*vee gehts*
Well, thanks.	Gut, danke.	*goot dahng-keh*
So-so.	Es geht.	*ehs geht*
Not bad.	Nicht schlecht.	*neeHt shleh-Ht*
And (how are) you?	Und Ihnen?	*oont ee-nen*
Good-bye.	Auf Wiedersehen.	*owf vee-dehr-zehn*
Bye.	Tschüß.	*tshews*
See you later.	Bis später.	*bihs shpay-ter*
I come from …	Ich komme aus …	*eeH koh-meh ows …*
America	Amerika	*ah-meh-ree-kah*
the United States	den Vereinig-ten Staaten	*dehn fer-ie-neeH-ten shtah-ten*
Canada	Kanada	*kah-nah-dah*
Where do you come from?	Woher kommen Sie?	*voh-bair kohmen zee*

"Do You Mind If I Ask You …?"

When you're first getting acquainted with someone, it's natural to have a lot of questions. To help you find out more about new people you meet, you'll use question words, or interrogative pronouns. Table 3.2 lists some of the question words you need to know.

Table 3.2   Question Words

English	German	Pronunciation
how	wie	*vee*
how many / how much	wie viele / wieviel	*vee <u>fee</u>-leh* / *vee-<u>feel</u>*
what	was	*vahs*
when	wann	*vahn*
where	wo	*voh*
who	wer	*vair*
why	warum	*vah-room*

A Little About Yourself

Just as you'll have questions about the people you meet, they'll have questions for you, too. The following tables will help you talk about yourself, what you like to do, and your family.

Before you start telling about yourself, you need to know a little about the verb "to have," or *haben*. *Haben* is essential to talking about yourself, particularly when it comes to describing your family, and Table 3.3 gives you some forms you might need.

Table 3.3 Different Forms of *Haben* ("To Have")

English	German	Pronunciation
I have a ...	Ich habe einen / eine ...*	eeH *hah*-beh *ie*-nen / *ie*-ne ...
I have (no) siblings.	Ich habe (keine) Geschwister.	eeH *hah*-be (*kie*-ne) geh-*shvees*-ter
Do you have a ...?	Haben Sie einen / eine ...?*	*hah*-ben zee *ie*-nen / *ie*-ne ...
He / She has (two) ...	Er / Sie hat (zwei) ...	air / zee haht (*tsvie*) ...
We have ...	Wir haben ...	veer *hah*-ben ...
They have ...	Sie haben ...	zee *hah*-ben ...

What's This?

*Remember to use *einen* if the word following the "have" verb is masculine, *eine* if it's feminine, and *ein* if the word is neuter. For more information on word gender, see Table 15.1.

"I _____ for a Living"

When you meet someone new, it normally doesn't take long for the subject of professions, or *Berufe* (*beh-roo-feh*), to come up. In case someone asks you what your job is, Table 3.4 prepares you to answer.

Table 3.4   Types of Jobs

English	German	Pronunciation
I am a …	Ich bin …	*eeH bin …*
Are you a …?	Sind Sie …?	*zeent zee …*
I work for a …	Ich arbeite für einen / eine …*	*eeH <u>ahr</u>-bie-teh fewr <u>ie</u>-nen / <u>ie</u>-neh*
Do you work for a …?	Arbeiten Sie für einen / eine …?*	*<u>ahr</u>-bie-ten zee fewr <u>ie</u>-nen / <u>ie</u>-ne …*
accountant	Buchhalter (m.) Buchhalterin (f.)	*<u>bookh</u>-hahl-ter* *<u>bookh</u>-hahl-ter-in*
craftsperson	Handwerker (m.) Handwerkerin (f.)	*<u>hahnd</u>-ver-ker* *<u>hahnd</u>-ver-ker-in*
dentist	Zahnarzt (m.) Zahnärztin (f.)	*<u>tsahn</u>-artst* *<u>tsahn</u>-airts-tin*
engineer	Ingenieur (m.) Ingenieurin (f.)	*in-dsheh-<u>nyewr</u>* *in-dsheh-<u>nyeur</u>-in*
entrepreneur	Unternehmer (m.) Unternehmerin (f.)	*oon-ter-<u>neh</u>-mer* *oon-ter-<u>neh</u>-mer-in*
government employee	Beamter (m.) Beamtin (f.)	*beh-<u>ahm</u>-ter* *beh-<u>ahm</u>-tin*
lawyer	Rechtsanwalt (m.) Rechtsanwältin (f.)	*<u>rayHts</u>-ahn-valt* *<u>rayHts</u>-ahn-veil-tin*
manager	Manager (m.) Managerin (f.)	*<u>meh</u>-neh-dsher* *<u>meh</u>-neh-dsher-in*
nurse	Krankenpfleger (m.) Krankenschwester (f.)	*<u>krahn</u>-ken-pflay-gher;* *<u>krahn</u>-ken-shves-ter*
physician	Arzt (m.) Ärztin (f.)	*artst* *<u>airts</u>-tin*
police officer	Polizist (m.) Polizistin (f.)	*poh-lee-<u>tsist</u>* *poh-lee-<u>tsis</u>-tin*

continues

Table 3.4   Types of Jobs (continued)

English	German	Pronunciation
salesperson	Kaufmann (m.)	*kowf-mahn*
	Kauffrau (f.)	*kowf-frow*
secretary	Sekretär (m.)	*zeh-kreh-tair*
	Sekretärin (f.)	*zeh-kreh-tair-in*
teacher	Lehrer (m.)	*leh-rer*
	Lehrerin (f.)	*leh-reh-rin*

What's This?

In German, most professions exist in a masculine and a feminine form, depending on whether the person holding the job is a man or a woman. Often, you only have to add *-in* to obtain the feminine form.

"For Fun, I Like to _____"

Just as important as what you do for work is what you do for fun. Table 3.5 will help you express the activities you enjoy. To say you don't enjoy something, add *Don't* or *nicht* (*neeHt*) at the end of the sentence.

Table 3.5   Leisure Activities

English	German	Pronunciation
I (don't) like to dance.	Ich tanze (nicht) gern.	*eeH <u>tahn</u>-tseh (neeHt) gayrn*
I like to play ...*	Ich spiele gern ...*	*eeH <u>shpee</u>-leh gayrn ...*
I like to read.	Ich lese gern.	*eeH <u>leh</u>-zeh gayrn*
I like to go shopping.	Ich gehe gern einkaufen.	*eeH <u>geh</u>-eh gayrn <u>ien</u>-kow-fen*
I like to do crafts.	Ich bastele gern.	*eeH <u>bah</u>-steh-leh gayrn*
I like to do sports.	Ich mache gern Sport.	*eeH <u>mah</u>-khe gayrn shpohrt*
I like to swim.	Ich schwimme gern.	*eeH <u>shvih</u>-meh gayrn*
I like to travel.	Ich verreise gern.	*eeH feh-<u>rie</u>-zeh gayrn*
I like art.	Ich mag Kunst.	*eeH mahk koonst*
I like music.	Ich mag Musik.	*eeH mahk moo-<u>zeek</u>*
I like nature.	Ich mag die Natur.	*eeH mahk dee nah-<u>toor</u>*
I like (to watch) sports.	Ich mag Sport.**	*eeH mahk shpohrt*

What's This?

**Most sports and many instruments are very similar or identical in German and in English, for example Tennis and Basketball or *Trompete* and *Violine*. Two exceptions are soccer, which is *Fußball* (*foos-bahl*) and piano, which is *Klavier* (*klah-veer*). Football is called *American Football*.

Introducing Your Family

If you're traveling with your family, you'll want to be able to introduce them to the people you meet. Tables 3.6 through 3.9 will help you make introductions.

Table 3.6 Masculine Relatives

English	German	Pronunciation
This is my ...	Das ist mein ...	*dahs ist mien ...*
This is the ...	Das ist der ...	*dahs ist dair ...*
of ...	von ...	*fohn ...*
father	Vater	*fah-ter*
grandfather	Großvater	*grohs-fah-ter*
brother	Bruder	*broo-der*
son	Sohn	*zohn*
grandson	Enkel	*ayng-kel*
uncle	Onkel	*ohng-kel*
cousin	Cousin	*koo-zayng*
nephew	Neffe	*nay-feh*
husband	Mann	*mahn*
boyfriend	Freund	*froynt*
His name is ...	Er heißt ...	*air hiest ...*

Table 3.7   Feminine Relatives

English	German	Pronunciation
This is my ...	Das ist meine ...	*dahs ist __mie__-neh* ...
This is the ... of ...	Das ist die ... von ...	*dahs ist dee ... fohn* ...
mother	Mutter	*__moo__-ter*
grandmother	Großmutter	*__grohs__-moo-ter*
sister	Schwester	*__shvays__-ter*
daughter	Tochter	*__tohkh__-ter*
granddaughter	Enkelin	*__ayn__-keh-lin*
aunt	Tante	*__tahn__-teh*
cousin	Cousine	*koo-__zee__-neh*
niece	Nichte	*__neeH__-teh*
wife	Frau	*frow*
girlfriend	Freundin	*__froyn__-din*
Her name is ...	Sie heißt ...	*zee hiest* ...

Table 3.8   Neuter and Plural Relatives

English	German	Pronunciation
This is my child.	Das ist mein Kind.	*dahs ist mien kihnt*
These are my ... children.	Das sind meine ... Kinder.	*dahs zint __mie__-ne ... __kihn__-der*
parents	Eltern	*__ayl__-tern*
grandparents	Großeltern	*__grohs__-ayl-tern*
Their names are ...	Sie heißen ...	*zee __hie__-sen* ...

Table 3.9   Asking About Relatives

English	German	Pronunciation
Is that your …?	Ist das Ihr …?	*ist dahs eer …*
What is his name?	Wie heißt er?	*vee hiest air*
What is her name?	Wie heißt sie?	*vee hiest zee*
What are their names?	Wie heißen sie?	*vee hie-sen zee*
How old is he / she?	Wie alt ist er / sie?	*vee ahlt ist air / zee*

Getting Better Acquainted

German people tend to be more reserved and less familiar with one another than Americans are. As you get to know the people you meet better, however, you'll probably find that they become more receptive and open.

When you know people more intimately, you may be offered the informal *du* instead of the formal *Sie* when addressing them. Table 3.10 will help you understand the familiar address of "you," or *du*.

Table 3.10   The Familiar "You"

English	German	Pronunciation
Please call me (your first name).	Bitte sagen Sie … zu mir.	*bee-teh zah-ghen zee … tsoo meer*
Please say "du" to me.	Bitte sag "du" zu mir.	*bee-teh zahg doo tsoo meer*
What is your name?	Wie heißt du?	*vee hiest doo*

Watch It!

There are generational and cultural differences in the use of the informal "you" in Germany and other European countries. As a general rule, use *du* ("you") only after you've been asked to, or for children and your family members. Otherwise, use the formal *Sie*. Expect to call people by their last names until they've asked you to use their first names. And while you're still getting acquainted, you should introduce yourself with your first and last name.

Generally, you'll find German people to be friendly and willing to help you if you stumble in some of your attempts to communicate. The important thing is to keep trying and be open to conversing with the people you meet.

Chapter 4

Traveling in Germany

In This Chapter

- Traveling in Germany
- Knowing how to find the transportation you want
- Renting a car
- Understanding road signs
- Asking for directions

Regardless of how you choose to travel in Germany, you're apt to be impressed with the country's transportation system. Austria, Germany, and Switzerland are known for their efficient travel systems, both in the cities and across the country. Road, train, and air travel are well run and reliable.

Finding Your Way in a Foreign Land

Tables 4.1 and 4.2 give you the phrases you need to find, buy tickets for, and board a source of public transportation.

Table 4.1   Finding Transportation

English	German	Pronunciation
Where is ...?	Wo ist ...?	*voh ist ...*
the (nearest) bus stop	die (nächste) Bus-haltestelle	*dee (nayks-teh) boos-hahl-teh-shteh-leh*
the subway (station)	die U-Bahn (Station)	*dee oo-bahn (shtah-tsyohn)*
the taxi stand	der Taxistand	*dair tahk-see-shtahnt*
the train station	der Bahnhof	*dair bahn-hohf*
the light rail to ...	die Straßenbahn nach ...	*dee shtrah-sen-bahn nahkh ...*
the bus to ...	der Bus nach ...	*dair boos nahkh ...*
the subway to ...	die U-Bahn nach ...	*dee oo-bahn nahkh ...*
the train to ...	der Zug nach ...	*dair tsook nahkh ...*

Table 4.2   Getting Ready to Board

English	German	Pronunciation
Where can I buy a ticket?	Wo kann ich eine Fahrkarte kaufen?	*voh kahn eeH ie-ne fahr-kahr-teh kow-fen*
How much is a ticket to ...?	Wieviel kostet eine Fahrkarte nach ...?	*vee-feel kohs-tet ie-ne fahr-kahr-teh nahkh ...*
How many stops are there between here and ...?	Wieviele Halte-stellen liegen zwischen hier und ...?	*vee-fee-leh hahl-teh-shteh-len lee-ghen tsvee-shen heer oont ...*
(How often) do I have to change trains?	(Wie oft) muss ich umsteigen?	*(vee ohft) moos eeH oom-shtie-ghen*
From which platform does (the train) leave?	Von welchem Gleis fährt (der Zug) ab?	*fohn vayl-Hem glice fayrt (dair tsook) ahp*

English	German	Pronunciation
One ticket to ..., please.	Eine Fahrkarte nach ..., bitte.	*ie-ne fahr-kahr-teh nahkh ... bee-teh*
one way	einfach	*ien-fahkh*
round trip	hin und zurück	*heen oont tsoo-rewk*
one adult	ein Erwachsener	*ien air-vahk-seh-ner*
two adults	zwei Erwachsene	*tsvie air-vahk-seh-neh*
one child	ein Kind	*ien keent*
two children	zwei Kinder	*tsvie keen-der*
(non)smoking	(Nicht) Raucher	*(neeHt) row-kher*
first / second class, please	erste / zweite Klasse, bitte	*airs-teh / tsvie-teh klah-seh bee-teh*
arrival	die Ankunft	*dee ahn-koonft*
departure	die Abfahrt	*dee up-fahrt*

While We're at It

> While checking out public transportation schedules, remember that all times in Germany are given using the 24-hour system, sometimes called "military time." See Chapter 6 for time phrases.

Asking for Help While Traveling

When you've made it to and boarded your train, bus, or subway, you might find that you need to ask the driver, conductor, or other passengers for help. Table 4.3 gives you phrases you need to do so.

Table 4.3 Asking for Help

English	German	Pronunciation
Is this the (train) to ...?	Ist das der Zug nach ...?	*ist dahs dair tsook nahkh ...*
I would like to go to ...	Ich möchte nach ...	*eeH murH-teh nahkh ...*
I would like to get off at the ...	Ich möchte am / an der ... aussteigen.	*eeH murH-teh ahm / ahn dair ... ows-shtie-ghen*
How many more stops are there to ...?	Wieviele Halte-stellen sind es noch bis ...?	*vee-fee-leh hahl-teh-shteh-len seent ehs nohH bihs ...*
What is the next station called?	Wie heißt die nächste Station?	*vee hiest dee nayks-the shtah-tsyohn*
Where is there a map?	Wo gibt es eine Karte?	*voh geebt ehs ie-neh kahr-the*
Is this seat free?	Ist dieser Sitz frei?	*ist dee-zehr zits frie*

What's This?

Use *am* ("at the") for a masculine or neuter (*der* or *das*) landmark; use *an der* ("at the") for a feminine (*die*) one. For a list of landmarks, see Chapter 7.

Taxi Talk

Taxis are plentiful in Germany and are often found at taxi stands, where drivers wait for customers. Most German taxis are cream-colored with a yellow and black Taxi sign. And all cabs are metered, so you'll be able to see your fare when you reach your destination. It's customary to round up your fare to the nearest euro as a tip, adding more if you had particularly heavy luggage—or a great deal. The phrases in Table 4.4 will help you summon a cab and communicate with your driver.

Table 4.4 Getting a Cab

English	German	Pronunciation
Can you please call me a cab?	Können Sie mir bitte ein Taxi rufen?	_kur_-nen zee meer _bee_-teh ien _tahk_-see _roo_-fen
How much is it to the ... hotel?	Wieviel kostet es zum / zur ...?	_vee_-feel _kohs_-tet ehs tsoom / tsoor ...
I would like to go to the ...	Ich möchte zum / zur ...	eeH _murH_-teh tsoom / tsoor ...
Stop here!	Halten Sie hier an!	_hahl_-ten zee heer ahn
Wait for me!	Warten Sie auf mich!	_vahr_-ten zee owf meeH

What's This?

If you are headed for a place in town, such as a particular hotel, use _zu_ to express "to." Use _zum_ (meaning "to the") for masculine or neuter sites (_der_ or _das_ words) and _zur_ for feminine sites (_die_ words). For a list of places in town, check out Chapter 7.

Driving a Car in Germany

If you choose to rent a car, you'll probably be pleased with central Europe's highway system. It's important to realize, however, that driving a car in Europe is quite different from driving in North America. The streets tend to be narrower, and the traffic denser and faster. Many traffic signs look entirely different from the ones we have in America, and many European countries have strict rules about the right of way and parking.

 While We're at It _____

> Germany's audacious highway, the _Autobahn,_ is renowned for having no general speed limit, but don't hit the gas pedal just yet. Varying speed limits are posted along nearly all parts of it. In Austria and Switzerland, you must have a special toll sticker on your car to use the highways.

Procuring a Car

Most major U.S. and European car rental agencies are found in Germany as well, and rental cars are available in Germany at all airports and many of the larger rail stations. If you decide to wait until you get to Germany to rent a car, Table 4.5 contains phrases that will help you get one.

Table 4.5 Renting a Car

English	German	Pronunciation
I would like (to rent) …	Ich möchte …	*eeH murH-teh …*
a car	ein Auto mieten	*ien ow-toh mee-ten*
a (make of car)	einen (…) mieten	*ie-nen … mee-ten*
I would like a car …	Ich möchte ein Auto …	*eeH murH-teh ien ow-toh …*
with automatic transmission	mit Automatik	*mit ow-toh-mah-tik*
with manual transmission	mit Gangschaltung	*mit gahng-shahl-toong*
How much does it cost …?	Wieviel kostet es …?	*vee-feel kobs-tet ehs …*
per day	pro Tag	*proh tahk*
per week	pro Woche	*proh voh-He*
per kilometer	pro Kilometer	*proh kee-loh-meh-ter*
How much is the insurance?	Wieviel kostet die Versicherung?	*vee-feel kobs-tet dee fer-see-Her-oong*
Is that including the gas?	Ist das inklusive Benzin?	*ist dahs een-kloo-zee-veh behn-tseen*
Do you accept credit cards?	Nehmen Sie Kreditkarten?	*neh-men zee kreh-deet-kahr-ten*
Do you fill it up with gas?	Tanken Sie es voll?	*tahng-ken zee ehs fohl*

Understanding Road Signs and Traffic Rules

Most European traffic signs are obscure to the uninitiated, with meanings that can't be easily interpreted. Table 4.6 will help you decipher some common signs.

Table 4.6 Common Road Signs

English	German	Pronunciation
border crossing	Zoll	*tsohl*
deviation	Umleitung	*oom-lie-toong*
one-way street	Einbahnstraße	*ien-bahn-shtrah-seh*
under wet conditions	bei Nässe	*by nay-seh*
under icy conditions	bei Glatteis	*by glaht-ice*
parking garage	das Parkhaus die Tiefgarage	*dahs park-house* *dee teef-gah-rah-she*
parking lot	der Parkplatz	*dair park-plahts*
with parking disk	mit Parkscheibe	*mit park-shie-beh*
weekdays	an Wochentagen	*ahn voh-khen-tah-ghen*
weekends	an Wochenenden	*ahn voh-khen-ehn-dehn*
on Sundays and holidays	an Sonn- und Feiertagen	*ahn zohn oont fie-er-tah-ghen*

Some parking lot signs will let you park for free for a limited time, but you must display a parking disc, or *Parkscheibe*. (You should find one of these blue-and-white paper discs in your rental car.) When you park, you set the time of your arrival on the disc, rounding up to the next half hour. At the end of the allotted parking time, you must have returned and—technically—moved your car.

Watch It!

You're heading for serious trouble if you don't heed Germany's fundamental traffic rule, the "right before left" rule. At every unmarked intersection, the car coming from the right automatically has priority over the car approaching from the left. That means the car on the right doesn't need to stop at all, even if it didn't arrive first at the intersection.

Asking for Directions (Even If You're a Man)

Whether you're walking around in town or trying to find your way by car, you'll likely have to ask for directions at some point. (Yes, men, you can stop and ask!) If you try to speak German when speaking to natives, they'll always appreciate your effort. When you're traveling off the beaten track, speaking German might very well be your only option. Table 4.7 will help you out when you need to ask for directions.

Table 4.7 Asking for Directions

English	German	Pronunciation
Excuse me, I'm looking for ...	Entschuldigung, ich suche ...	ehnt-_shool_-dee-goong eeH _soo_-khe ...
Do you know the way?	Wissen Sie den Weg?	_vih_-sen zee dehn vehk
Is this the way to ...?	Geht es hier nach / zu ...?	gayt ehs heer nahkh / tsoo ...
straight ahead	geradeaus	geh-_rah_-deh-ows
to the left	nach links	nahkh links
to the right	nach rechts	nahkh rayHts
to the north	nach Norden	nahkh _nohr_-den
to the south	nach Süden	nahkh s-ew-den
to the east	nach Osten	nahkh _ohs_-ten
to the west	nach Westen	nahkh _vehs_-ten
turn!	Biegen Sie ab!	_bee_-gen zee up
Drive / walk to (the first street)!	Fahren / Gehen Sie bis (zur ersten Straße)!	_fah_-ren / _geh_-ehn zee bis (tsoor _airs_-ten _shtrah_-seh)
Cross ...!	Überqueren Sie ...!	ew-ber-_kvay_-ren zee ...
Keep driving / walking!	Fahren / Gehen Sie weiter!	_fah_-ren / _geh_-ehn zee _vie_-ter
at the intersection	an der Kreuzung	ahn dair _kroy_-tsoong
at the traffic light	an der Ampel	ahn dair _ahm_-pehl
at the (traffic) sign	am (Verkehrs-)Schild	ahm (fer-_kayrs_-)shihlt

Finding your way around a foreign land can be a bit daunting, but traveling in Germany needn't be that difficult once you've nailed a few key phrases to help you find your way and get the transporation you need. So relax and enjoy the scenery!

Chapter 5

At the Hotel

In This Chapter

- Lodging in Germany
- Checking in
- Finding your floor
- Navigating the hotel
- Asking for what you need
- Remembering your manners

An exciting part of any trip is checking out the hotel where you'll be staying. Germany, Austria, and Switzerland boast many hotels, inns, and guesthouses in a variety of styles and with a range of prices.

German hotels are given star rating designations, based on unified criteria. Tourist information centers (called *Touristeninformation* or *Verkehrsbüro*) can help you find a hotel that meets your needs. These centers are located in larger airports, train stations, and in town centers.

Lodging in Germany

Accommodations in Germany, Austria, and Switzerland range from lavishly appointed hotels to simple youth hostels. You will, of course, have to determine which type of lodging is right for you.

 While We're at It _____

> People of any age can stay inexpensively in Germany's youth hostels. The official association of German youth hostels is called *Deutsches Jugendherbergswerk*, or *DJH*.

Table 5.1 lists some accommodations-related words to help you find the best place to stay.

Table 5.1   Types of Lodging

English	German	Pronunciation
hotel	das Hotel	*dahs hoh-tel*
hotel offering only breakfast	das Hotel Garni	*dahs hoh-tel gahr-nee*
inn	das Gästehaus	*dahs guest-eh-house*
motel	das Motel	*dahs moh-tel*
bed and breakfast	die Pension	*dee pehn-zyohn*
youth hostel	die Jugendherberge	*dee yoo-ghend-hehr-behr-ghe*

While We're at It

If you are staying at a hotel, the price of breakfast is normally included in your nightly rate. You sometimes can take other meals there as well, if you want.

Checking In and Checking Out

After you've decided on the type of lodging you want, you'll be ready to check in at the hotel or inn of your choice. Although most hotel owners and managers—even in smaller establishments—speak English, it's still good to be aware of the German phrases listed in Table 5.2 that might come in handy.

Table 5.2   Checking In and Out of a Hotel

English	German	Pronunciation
Do you have a room (with ...) available?	Haben Sie ein Zimmer (mit ...) frei?	*hah-ben zee ien tsih-mer (mit ...) frie*
What does the room cost (per night)?	Wieviel kostet das Zimmer (pro Nacht)?	*vee-feel kohs-tet dahs tsih-mehr (proh nakht)*
At what time can I check in?	Um wieviel Uhr kann ich das Zimmer beziehen?	*oom vee-feel oor kahn eeH dahs tsih-mer beh-tsee-ehn*
At what time do I need to check out?	Um wieviel Uhr muß ich das Zimmer verlassen?	*oom vee-feel oor moos eeH dahs tsih-mer fer-lah-sen*

continues

Table 5.2 Checking In and Out of a Hotel
(continued)

English	German	Pronunciation
room number	Zimmer Nummer	_tsih_-mer _noo_-mer
On which story is …?	Auf welcher Etage ist …?	owf _vayl_-Her eh-_tah_-sheh ist …
The bill, please.	Die Rechnung, bitte.	dee _rehH_-noong _bee_-teh
Can I pick up my luggage later?	Kann ich mein Gepäck später abholen?	kahn eeH mien geh-_payk_ _shpay_-ter _up_-hoh-len
I would like to stay another night (two more nights).	Ich möchte noch eine Nacht (zwei Nächte) bleiben.	eeH _murH_-teh nohkh _ie_-ne nakht (tsvie _nayH_-te) _blie_-ben

"Which Floor Is My Room On?"

Locating your room in a European hotel isn't the same as in the United States because floor levels are numbered differently. Germans begin counting floors only above street level. So what we would think of as the second floor in the United States is considered the first floor in Germany.

Don't worry, though. If you get confused, just use the phrases in Table 5.3 to ask someone for help.

Table 5.3   Finding Your Floor

English	German	Pronunciation
Which story, please?	Welche Etage, bitte?	_vehl_-He eh-_tah_-sheh _bee_-teh
basement	das Untergeschoss	dahs _oon_-ter-geh-shohs
level 1	das Erdgeschoss	dahs _aird_-geh-shohs
level 2	der erste Stock	dair _airs_-teh shtohk
level 3	der zweite Stock	dair _tsvie_-teh shtohk

Finding Your Way Around the Hotel

When you've found your room and settled in, you'll probably want to check out the hotel facilities. Table 5.4 will help you locate the places and people you want to find.

Table 5.4   Asking About the Hotel's Facilities

English	German	Pronunciation
Is there ...?	Gibt es ...?	geebt ehs
air conditioning	eine Klimaan-lage	_ie_-ne _klee_-mah-ahn-lah-ghe
a bar	eine Bar	_ie_-ne bar
a bellman	einen Pagen	_ie_-nen _pah_-shehn
conference center	Konferenzsäle	kohn-fay-_rents_-say-leh
a caretaker / janitor	einen Hausmeister	_ie_-nen _house_-mie-ster
a doorman	einen Portier	_ie_-nen poor-_tee-ay_
an elevator	einen Aufzug einen Lift	_ie_-nen _owf_-tsook _ie_-nen lift
a fitness center	ein Fitness Center	ien _fitness_ tsen-tehr

continues

Table 5.4 Asking About the Hotel's Facilities

(continued)

English	German	Pronunciation
a gift shop	eine Geschenk-boutique	*ie-ne geh-shank-boo-teek*
maid service	Zimmerservice	*tsih-mehr-service*
a restaurant	ein Restaurant	*ien rest-oh-rah*
a staircase	ein Treppenhaus	*ien trap-ehn-house*
stairs	eine Treppe	*ie-ne trap-eh*
a swimming pool	ein Schwimmbad	*ien shveem-bahd*
a valet	einen Wagen-meister	*ie-nen vah-ghehn-mies-ter*

Asking for What You Need

You'll probably discover something you need or want during your stay at a German hotel or inn. Although most facilities are well supplied, you never know when you might want an extra pillow or a bucket of ice cubes. Table 5.5 will make it easy for you to express your wants and needs.

Table 5.5 Hotel Wants and Needs

English	German	Pronunciation
I need ...	Ich brauche ...	*eeH brow-khe ...*
I would like to have ...	Ich hätte gern ...	*eeH het-eh gayrn ...*
air conditioning	Klimaanlage	*klee-mah-ahn-lah-ghe*
an ashtray	einen Aschen-becher	*ie-nen ah-shen-beh-Her*

English	German	Pronunciation
I need …	Ich brauche …	*eeH brow-khe …*
I would like to have …	Ich hätte gern …	*eeH het-eh gayrn …*
a balcony	einen Balkon	*ie-nen bahl-kohn*
a bathroom	ein Badezimmer	*ien bah-deh-tsih-mer*
a blanket	eine Decke	*ie-ne deh-keh*
a hair dryer	einen Fön	*ie-nen furn*
a hanger	einen Kleider-haken	*ie-nen klie-der-hah-ken*
a key	einen Schlüssel	*ie-nen shlew-sel*
ice cubes	Eiswürfel	*ice-vewr-fel*
one / two warm meals per day	Halbpension / Vollpension	*hahlb-pehn-syohn / fohl-pehn-syohn*
mineral water	Mineralwasser	*mee-nay-rahl-vah-ser*
a room onto the courtyard	ein Zimmer zum Hof	*ien tsih-mer tsoom hohf*
onto the sea	zum Meer	*tsoom mehr*
onto the garden	zum Garten	*tsoom gahr-ten*
a pillow	ein Kissen	*ien kiss-en*
a safe-deposit box	einen Safe	*ie-nen safe*
a shower	eine Dusche	*ie-ne doo-sheh*
a single / double room	ein Einzelzimmer / Doppelzimmer	*ien-tsel-tsih-mer / doh-pel-tsih-mer*
a telephone	ein Telefon	*ien teh-leh-fohn*
a television	einen Fernseher	*ie-nen fayrn-zeh-ehr*
tissues	Taschentücher	*tah-shehn-tew-Hehr*
toilet paper	Toilettenpapier	*toy-let-ehn-pah-peer*
a towel	ein Handtuch	*ien hahn-tookh*
a beach towel	ein Badetuch	*ien bah-deh-tookh*
a transformer	einen Trafo	*ie-nen trah-foe*

While We're at It

Hotels and restaurants always include their service charge on your bill, which is sufficient for most tips. You should, however, tip bellhops and porters 1 euro for each service, and it's customary to leave 1 euro per night for hotel cleaning personnel. If you receive exceptional service from the desk clerk, you can consider tipping there as well, although it's not necessary.

Remembering Your Manners

Regardless of where or for what purpose you travel, you represent your own country. Whether they're deserved or not, many people in other countries have negative stereotypes about Americans, thinking them to be rude and pushy. Remembering the phrases in Table 5.6, however, will help you dispel those attitudes and impress the Germans with whom you come into contact.

Table 5.6   Politeness

English	German	Pronunciation
Excuse me. / Pardon.	Entschuldigung.	*ehn-tshool-dee-goong*
Please.	Bitte.	*bee-teh*
Thank you.	Danke.	*dahng-keh*
	Dankeschön.	*dahng-keh-shurn*

English	German	Pronunciation
Thanks a lot.	Vielen Dank.	_fee_-len dahnk
You're welcome. / Here you are.	Bitte.	_bee_-teh
Don't mention it.	Gern geschehen.	gayrn geh-_shayn_

Germany's many hotels and inns provide a wide variety of accommodation choices. Whatever type of lodging you choose, the phrases included in this chapter will help you to deal with the situations you encounter there.

Let's Get Basic: Weather, Time, and Dates

In This Chapter

- Talking about the weather
- Converting Celsius to Fahrenheit
- Learning the days of the week
- Checking out months and seasons
- Knowing how to ask and give the date
- Understanding the 24-hour time system

You must be prepared to discuss certain topics regardless of where you travel. Whether your treks take you to Germany, Japan, or Ethiopia, you need to be able to communicate about weather, dates, and time.

Knowing What Weather to Expect

The weather in Germany, Austria, and Switzerland is comparable to that of the eastern United States.

That is, it varies from region to region, and can be, shall we say, a bit unpredictable. So be sure to include some rain gear and a warm sweater or two when you pack for your trip.

Table 6.1 includes many phrases that will help you discuss the weather with confidence.

Table 6.1 Weather Expressions

English	German	Pronunciation
What is the weather like (tomorrow)?	Wie ist das Wetter (morgen)?	*vee ist dahs* *vet-ah* *(morgan)*
The weather is beautiful.	Das Wetter ist schön.	*dahs vet-ah ist shurn*
It is beautiful.	Es ist schön.	*ehs ist shurn*
It is (too) hot.	Es ist (zu) heiß.	*ehs ist (tsoo) hies*
It is sunny.	Es ist sonnig.	*ehs ist zon-iH*
It is bad weather.	Es ist schlecht.	*ehs ist shlayHt*
It is (not) cold.	Es ist (nicht) kalt.	*ehs ist (neeHt) kahlt*
It is cool.	Es ist kühl.	*ehs ist kewl*
It is foggy.	Es ist neblig.	*ehs ist nay-bliH*
It is windy.	Es ist windig.	*ehs ist vin-diH*
It is overcast.	Es ist bedeckt.	*ehs ist beh-deck-t*
It is raining.	Es regnet.	*ehs rayg-net*
It is snowing.	Es schneit.	*ehs shniet*
It has snowed.	Es hat geschneit.	*ehs haht geh-shniet*
It is humid.	Es ist schwül.	*ehs ist shvurl*
It is hailing.	Es hagelt.	*ehs hah-gaylt*
There is thunder and lightning.	Es donnert und blitzt.	*ehs don-ert oont blitst*
There will be a thunderstorm.	Es gibt ein Gewitter.	*ehs geebt ien geh-vit-er*

English	German	Pronunciation
What's the temperature? (How many degrees is it?)	Wieviel Grad ist es?	_vee-feel grahd ist ehs_
It is forty degrees.	Es ist vierzig Grad.	_ehs ist feer-tsiH grahd_
It is minus ten degrees.	Es ist minus zehn Grad.	_ehs ist mee-noos tsehn grahd_

What's All This Talk About Celsius?

In Europe and most other parts of the world, temperatures are measured in degrees Celsius, rather than on the Fahrenheit scale used in the United States. You might find it a little tricky to convert the Celsius temperature to Fahrenheit at first, but you'll soon learn to estimate.

Use the benchmarks in Table 6.2 to help you estimate the temperature quickly.

Table 6.2   Temperature Conversions

Degrees Celsius	Degrees Fahrenheit
28°C = 82°F	
0	32
16	61
42	108
100	212

What's This?

In English, you might occasionally hear the word *Centigrade* in weather-related conversation, but don't be alarmed—it's the same as Celsius. Germans usually just say Grad (graht)—degrees—instead of Grad celsius.

Days of the Week

Days of the week and weather are definitely connected. After all, how often do you ask what the weather will be like on a particular day? Will it be warm on Sunday? Is it expected to rain this Wednesday?

While We're at It

Here's a tip for learning the days of the week: The German words for Monday, Friday, Saturday, and Sunday all begin with the same letters as their English counterparts.

Table 6.3 will help you learn and pronounce the days of the week. The common abbreviation for each day is included with the German word.

Table 6.3   Days of the Week

English	German (and Common Abbreviation)	Pronunciation
Monday	Montag (Mo)	_moan_-tahk
Tuesday	Dienstag (Di)	_deens_-tahk
Wednesday	Mittwoch (Mi)	_mit_-vohkh
Thursday	Donnerstag (Do)	_don_-ers-tahk
Friday	Freitag (Fr)	_fry_-tahk
Saturday	Samstag (Sa)	_zahms_-tahk
Sunday	Sonntag (So)	_zohn_-tahk

 While We're at It

Monday, not Sunday, is considered the first day of the German week. Monday is listed as the first day on a German calendar, too.

Months and Seasons

Just like days of the week, the months of the year and weather have many connections. For example, you'll want to know whether the region of Germany you'll be visiting gets snow in December or heavy rains during the fall months.

To help you ask about this, the months of the year are listed in Table 6.4 and the seasons in Table 6.5.

Table 6.4   Months of the Year

English	German	Pronunciation
January	Januar	_yah_-noo-ahr
February	Februar	_fay_-broo-ahr
March	März	mayr-ts
April	April	_ah_-pril
May	Mai	my
June	Juni	_yoo_-nee
July	Juli	_yoo_-lee
August	August	_ow_-goost
September	September	zep-_tem_-ber
October	Oktober	ohk-_toh_-ber
November	November	noh-_vem_-ber
December	Dezember	day-_tsem_-ber

The German pronunciations for the months are different from how we say them in English, even though the words themselves are strikingly similar and in some cases identical. The same goes for some of the seasons, which are listed in Table 6.5.

Table 6.5   Seasons of the Year

English	German	Pronunciation
Spring	Frühling	_frew_-ling
Summer	Sommer	_zoh_-mer
Fall	Herbst	_hair_-pst
Winter	Winter	_vin_-ter

As German words and phrases go, the months and seasons probably won't be difficult to recognize. Now let's move on to talking about dates and times.

What's the Date, Please?

In German-speaking countries, you will often find the date written as 13.5.05 or 17.11.2005. No, this doesn't mean Germans have added months to the calendar!

Germans write the day first, followed by the number of the month, followed by the last two or all four digits of the year, with periods to separate the day, month, and year. Table 6.6 tells you how to ask someone the date.

Table 6.6   Asking for the Date

English	German	Pronunciation
What day is it today?	Welcher Tag ist heute?	_vel_-Her tahk ist _hoy_-the
What is the date today?	Welches Datum ist heute?	_vel_-Hes _dah_-toom ist _hoy_-the
Is today (May first)?	Ist heute der (erste Mai)?	ist _hoy_-teh dair (_air_-ste my)

You'll also need to be prepared to tell someone what the date is or talk about a particular date as it pertains to an event. Table 6.7 presents some ways you can give the date.

Table 6.7 Telling Someone the Date

English	German	Pronunciation
Today is (May second).	Heute ist der (zweite Mai). Wir haben heute den (zweiten Mai).	*hoy-teh ist dair (tsvie-teh my) veer hah-ben hoy-teh dehn (tsvie-ten my)*
May 3, 1982	dritter Mai neunzehnhundertzwei-undachtzig	*drih-tehr my noyn-tsehn-hoon-dehrt-tsvie-oont-akh-tseek*
05/04/2008	vierter fünfter zweitausendacht	*feer-tehr fewnf-tehr tsvie-tau-zent-akht*
on May 5, 2009	am fünften Mai zweitausendneun	*ahm fewnf-ten my tsvie-tau-zent-noyn*

To give the date in German, you need to use *ordinal numbers* presented in Table 6.8. For most numbers up to 20, you only have to add *-ter* to the end of the number to turn a regular numeral, such as *vier* (four), into an or-dinal number. From 20 on up, add *-ster* to change a numeral into an ordinal number.

What's This?

Ordinal numbers are those used to express the order of something. *First, second, third, fourth,* and so on are ordinal numbers.

Table 6.8   Ordinal Numbers

English	German	Pronunciation
first	erster	*airs*-ter
second	zweiter	*tsvie*-ter
third	dritter	*drih*-ter
fourth	vierter	*feer*-ter
fifth	fünfter	*fewnf*-ter
sixth	sechster	*seks*-ter
seventh	siebter / siebenter	*seeb*-ter / *see*-ben-ter
eighth	achter	*ahkh*-ter
ninth	neunter	*noyn*-ter
tenth	zehnter	*tsehn*-ter
twentieth	zwanzig**ster**	*tsvahn*-tsik-ster
twenty-first	einundzwanzig-**ster**	*ien*-oont-tsvahn-tsik-ster
twenty-second	zweiundzwanzig-**ster**	*tsvie*-oont-tsvahn-tsik-ster
thirtieth	dreißig**ster**	*drie*-sig-ster

Telling Time, German Style

The 24-hour system, also known as military time, is commonly used in Europe, especially for official purposes such as flight schedules, invitations, or doctor appointments. If you're not familiar with the 24-hour system, don't be alarmed. It's not hard to figure out.

To quickly figure out P.M. times when using the 24-hour system, just subtract 12 from the time given. If someone tells you it's *23.00 Uhr*, deduct 12 from 23 to see that it's 11 P.M.

Instead of midnight being called 12:00, it's called 0.00, or 24.00. You move forward from there until noon, which is 12:00. But instead of starting over again with 1 P.M., you keep moving forward through the numbers until you arrive back to midnight. So 1 P.M. equals *13.00 Uhr* (o'clock). Five P.M. is *17.00 Uhr;* 8 P.M. is *20.00 Uhr;* and 11 P.M. is *23.00 Uhr.* Table 6.9 presents ways to talk about the time of day.

Table 6.9   Talking About the Time of Day

English	German	Pronunciation
It is one o'clock.	Es ist ein Uhr.	*ehs ist ien oor*
It is 2:05.	Es ist zwei Uhr fünf.	*ehs ist tsvie oor fewnf*
It is five minutes after two.	Es ist fünf nach zwei.	*ehs ist fewnf nahH tsvie*
It is 3:10.	Es ist drei Uhr zehn.	*ehs ist drie oor tsehn*
It is ten minutes after three.	Es ist zehn nach drei.	*ehs ist tsehn nahH drie*
It is 3:15.	Es ist drei Uhr fünfzehn.	*ehs ist drie oor <u>fewnf</u>-tsehn*
It is quarter past three.	Es ist Viertel nach drei.	*ehs ist <u>feer</u>-tel nahH drie*
It is 4:30.	Es ist vier Uhr dreißig.	*ehs ist feer oor <u>drie</u>-sik*
It is half past four.	Es ist halb fünf.	*ehs ist hahlp fewnf*
It is 5:45.	Es ist fünf Uhr fünfundvierzig.	*ehs ist fewnf oor <u>fewnf</u>-oont-<u>feer</u>-tsik*
It is quarter till six.	Es ist Viertel vor sechs.	*ehs ist <u>feer</u>-tel for seks*
It is 6:50.	Es ist sechs Uhr fünfundfünfzig.	*ehs ist seks oor <u>fewnf</u>-oont-<u>fewnf</u>-tsik*
It is ten till seven.	Es ist zehn vor sieben.	*ehs ist tsehn for <u>see</u>-ben*

English	German	Pronunciation
It is noon.	Es ist Mittag.	*ehs ist <u>mit</u>-ahk*
It is midnight.	Es ist Mitternacht.	*ehs ist <u>mit</u>-er-nahHt*

Notice that in German, you look ahead to the next full hour when giving the half hour. So *halb sechs* = 5:30, *halb sieben* = 6:30, *halb drei* = 2:30, and so forth.

It's important to be able to ask and tell the time. It's also important to have a handle on time expressions, such as "last night," "a week from today," and "the day before yesterday." Table 6.10 provides many handy phrases.

Table 6.10   Time Expressions

English	German	Pronunciation
today	heute	<u>boy</u>-teh
tomorrow	morgen	<u>mor</u>-gan
tonight	heute Abend heute Nacht	<u>boy</u>-teh <u>ah</u>-bent <u>boy</u>-teh nahkht
yesterday	gestern	<u>ghes</u>-turn
(three days) ago	vor (drei Tagen) (+ Dat.)	for (drie <u>tah</u>-ghen)
the day after tomorrow	übermorgen	<u>ew</u>-ber-morgan
the day before yesterday	vorgestern	<u>for</u>-ghes-tehrn
the day	der Tag	dair tahk
the evening	der Abend	dair <u>ah</u>-bent
the night	die Nacht	dee nahkht

continues

Table 6.10   Time Expressions (continued)

English	German	Pronunciation
during	während (+ Gen.)	_veh_-rent
from (Tuesday) to (Friday)	von (Dienstag) bis (Freitag) (+ Dat.)	fohn (_deens_-tahk) bihs (_frie_-tahk)
for (three days)	seit (drei Tagen) (+ Dat.)	ziet (drie _tah_-ghen)
an hour	eine Stunde	_ie_-ne _shtoon_-deh
in (three days)	in (drei Tagen) (+ Dat.)	in (drie _tah_-ghen)
last	letzten / letzte / letztes	_lets_-ten / _lets_-teh / _lets_-tehs
last night	gestern Abend	_ghes_-tern _ah_-bent
the month	der Monat	dair _moh_-naht
next	nächste	_nayks_-teh
the next day	der nächste Tag	dayr _nayks_-teh tahk
on the next day	am nächsten Tag	ahm _nayks_-ten tahk
since (Monday)	seit (Montag) (+ Dat.)	ziet (_mohn_-tahk)
the week	die Woche	dee _voh_-khe
the weekend	das Wochenende	dahs _voh_-khen-_ehn_-deh
a week from today	heute in einer Woche	_hoy_-teh in _ie_-ner _voh_-khe
the year	das Jahr	dahs yahr

Prepositions always require a certain case after them (see Chapter 15 for more information about prepositions). For time expressions, *vor*, *seit*, and *in* require the dative, but *während* requires the genitive. Table 6.11 will help you sort it out.

While We're at It

There's a distinction between *night* and *evening* in German. *Nacht,* or "night," refers to the time most people are sleeping. The word for the time after sundown and while most people are still awake is *Abend* or "evening."

Table 6.11 Required Case for Certain Prepositions

	Dative	Genitive
Masculine, singular	vor/seit/in **einem** Tag	während **eines** Tage**s**
	dem Abend	des Abend**s**
Feminine, singular	vor/seit/in **einer** Woche	während **einer** Woche
	der Nacht	**der** Nacht
Neuter, singular	vor/seit/in **einem** Jahr	während **eines** Jahr**es**
	dem Wochenende	des Wochenende**s**
Plural	vor/seit/in drei Stunden	während drei Stunden
	den Wochenende**n**	**der** Wochenende**n**

As you see, the case mainly shows if you use *ein* ("a"/"an"; "one") or *der, die, das* ("the") after the preposition.

Now you're prepared to discuss weather, days, months, seasons, dates, and times, so it's time to lighten up and talk about some fun stuff— exploring and sightseeing in Germany.

Chapter 7

Let's Get Out and See the Sights

In This Chapter

- Making sightseeing inquiries
- Asking about the places you want to see
- Pronouncing names of countries and cities
- Finding your way to sports events
- Expressing your opinion

Whether you're in Germany, Austria, or Switzerland for business or pleasure, you're sure to want to visit some of the varied attractions found within these countries.

You'll find castles and cathedrals that are more than a thousand years old, as well as museums, gardens, flea markets, and carnivals. If you have the opportunity, sample as many of the sights during your visit as you can.

Asking the Right Questions

To find the places you want to see, you need to know some important phrases that will help you inquire about sights, tickets, admissions, and so forth. Those phrases are listed in Table 7.1.

Table 7.1 General Sightseeing Inquiries

English	German	Pronunciation
What is there to see?	Was gibt es da zu sehen?	*vahs geebt ehs dah tsoo seh-ehn*
At what time does it open (close)?	Um wieviel Uhr öffnet (schließt) es?	*oom vee-feel oor ewf-net (shleest) ehs*
Where can I buy tickets (for)?	Wo kann ich Karten (für) ... kaufen?	*voh kahn eeH kahr-ten (fewr) ... kow-fen*
How much does the admission cost?	Wieviel kostet der Eintritt?	*vee-feel kohs-tet dair ien-triht*
for children	für Kinder	*fewr keen-der*
How old is the child?	Wie alt ist das Kind?	*vee ahlt ist dahs keent*
(seven) years old	(sieben) Jahre alt	*(see-ben) yah-re ahlt*
Is it all right to take pictures?	Darf man Fotos machen?	*dahrf mahn foh-tohs mah-khen*
I would like a guided tour (in English).	Ich möchte eine Führung (auf English).	*eeh murH-teh ie-ne few-roong (owf ehng-leesh)*
I / We would like to see ...	Ich möchte / Wir möchten ... sehen.	*eeH murH-teh / veer murH-ten ... seh-ehn*
Would you like to go there (to ...)?	Möchten Sie dorthin (zum / zur ...) gehen?	*murH-ten zee dohrt-hihn (tsoom / tsoor) geh-ehn*
Would you like to see (that)?	Möchten Sie (das) sehen?	*murH-ten zee (dahs) seh-ehn*

English	German	Pronunciation
How do you like (it)?	Wie finden Sie (es)?	*vee fihn-den zee (ehs)*
(special) exhibit	die (Sonder) ausstellung	*dee (zohn-der) ows-shteh-loong*

"How Do I Get to the ...?"

Depending on your interests, budget, and time schedule, you'll choose different sites to visit and explore. Many tourist sites are worth a look, as are beautiful cities and exciting sporting events.

Tourist Sites

Tourist sites you might want to see, and phrases asking how to find them, are listed in Table 7.2.

Table 7.2   Common Tourist Sites

English	German	Pronunciation
Where can I obtain a map?	Wo kann ich eine Karte bekommen?	*voh kahn eeH ie-ne kahr-teh beh-koh-men*
What is the way ...?	Wie geht es ...?	*vee gayt ehs ...*
Do you know the way ...?	Kennen Sie den Weg ...?	*keh-nen zee dehn vehk ...*
I would like to go ...	Ich möchte ...	*eeH murH-the ...*
to the amusement park	zum Vergnügungspark	*tsoom fer-gnew-goongs-park*
to the beach	zum Strand	*tsoom shtrahnd*

continues

Table 7.2 Common Tourist Sites (continued)

English	German	Pronunciation
to the carnival	zum Jahrmarkt	*tsoom yahr-mahrkt*
	zur Kirmes	*tsoor keer-mess*
to the castle (medieval castle)	zum Schloß	*tsoom shlohs*
	zur Burg	*tsoor boork*
to the cathedral	zum Dom	*tsoom dohm*
	zum Münster	*tsoom mewns-ter*
to the church	zur Kirche	*tsoor keer-Heh*
to the circus	zum Zirkus	*tsoom tseer-koos*
to the flea market	zum Flohmarkt	*tsoom floh-mahrkt*
to the fountain	zum Brunnen	*tsoom broo-nen*
to the garden	zum Garten	*tsoom gahr-ten*
to the mall	zum Einkaufs-zentrum	*tsoom ien-kowfs-tsen-troom*
to the movie theater	zum Kino	*tsoom kee-noh*
to the museum	zum Museum	*tsoom moo-zay-oom*
to the nightclub	zur Bar	*tsoor bar*
	zur Disko(thek)	*tsoor dees-koh (tehk)*
to the opera	zur Oper	*tsoor oh-per*
to the pub	zur Kneipe	*tsoor knie-peh*
to the public square	zum Platz	*tsoom plahts*
to the restaurant	zum Restaurant	*tsoom res-toh-rahn*
to the theater	zum Theater	*tsoom tay-ah-ter*
to the tourist information center	zum Verkehrsamt	*tsoom fer-kehrs-ahmt*
	zur Touristenin-formation	*tsoor too-rees-ten-een-for-mah-tsyohn*
to the zoo	zum Zoo	*tsoom tsoh*
	zum Tiergarten	*tsoom teer-gahr-ten*

While We're at It

Public squares are generally named, just as streets are, so you might want to use the name to be quite clear about where you want to go. For instance, say *"Zum Marktplatz, bitte"* ("To the market square, please") or *"Zum Schillerplatz, bitte"* ("to Schiller Square, please").

The preposition *zu* ("to") is always followed by the dative case. When you want to say "to the," *zu* contracts with *dem* or *der.* Table 7.3 gives you some examples.

Table 7.3 Other Prepositions That Require the Dative

	Contracted Form of *zu* + Definite Article ("to the")	*zu* + Indefinite Article ("to a/an")
Masculine	zum	zu einem
Feminine	zur	zu einer
Neuter	zum	zu einem
Plural	zu den	zu

Cities and Countries

If you ask a German-speaking person how to get to Munich, pronouncing *Munich* as we do in English, the person you ask might not understand where you want to go due to the differences in the English and German pronunciations of the city's name. Table 7.4 will help you find your way to some of the beautiful cities in Germany, Austria, and Switzerland.

Table 7.4   Place-Names

English	German	Pronunciation
Austria	Österreich	*ur-steh-rieH*
Cologne	Köln	*Kurln*
Brunswick	Braunschweig	*brown-shviek*
Germany	Deutschland	*doytsh-lahnt*
Graz	Graz	*grahts*
Leipzig	Leipzig	*liep-tseek*
Munich	München	*mewn-Hen*
Switzerland	die Schweiz	*dee shviets*
Vienna	Wien	*veen*
Zürich	Zürich	*tsew-reeH*

Sporting Events

Germans are very sports-minded, and sporting facilities are widespread throughout the country. More than 2 million people volunteer as coaches and officials in the German Sports Federation (*Deutscher Sportbund*), which organizes and runs sports groups throughout Germany. Soccer, which Europeans call football, is especially popular.

Table 7.5 will help you find your way to athletic events and recreational activities. As you'll see, many team sport names, including tennis, basketball, hockey, golf, and volleyball, are very similar or even the same in English and German.

Table 7.5 Sports and Recreation

English	German	Pronunciation
car race	das Autorennen	*dahs ow-toh-reh-nen*
bicycle race	das Radrennen	*dahs rahd-reh-nen*
hiking trail	der Wanderweg	*dair vahn-der-vayk*
horse race	das Pferderennen	*dahs pfair-deh-reh-nen*
ski-trail, cross-country	die Loipe	*dee loy-peh*
ski-trail, downhill	die Skipiste	*dee shee-pihs-teh*
(soccer) club	der (Fußball)verein	*dair (foos-bahl)fer-ien*
(soccer) match	das (Fußball)spiel	*dahs (foos-bahl)shpeel*
stadium	das Stadion	*dahs shtah-dee-ohn*

So How Did You Like It?

You've seen the sights, and now you want to express your opinions on the places you've been to. The phrases in Table 7.6 will enable you to do so.

Table 7.6   Expressing Your Opinion

English	German	Pronunciation
all right / so-so	Es geht	*ehs geht*
boring	langweilig	*lahng-vie-lihH*
(very) good	(sehr) gut	*(zayr) goot*
wonderful	wunderbar	*voon-der-bar*
I don't like (it).	(Es) gefällt mir nicht.	*(ehs) geh-fellt meer neeHt*
(It) doesn't interest me.	(Es) interessiert mich nicht.	*(ehs) ihn-treh-seert meeH neeHt*

 While We're at It _____

> For extensive information about tourist sites, travel, and culture in Germany, Switzerland, and Austria, check out www.about-germany.org.

Whether your tastes tend toward cultural events, historical landmarks, or sporting events, you'll find lots to do and see in Germany. In the next chapter, you'll learn phrases to help you with another sort of adventure in Germany—eating.

Chapter 8

Is It Time to Eat Yet?

In This Chapter

- Learning about different types of shops
- Reserving a table
- Food, food, and more food
- Being sure you get what you want
- Ordering a drink
- Finishing your meal

What's a vacation without some memorable meals? To get those meals, though, you need to know where to go and how to order the foods you want.

A Variety of Shops and Stores

Germany has a wonderful variety of shops and stores, all loaded with foods, drinks, and specialties you'll want to experience. Table 8.1 tells you the types of shops you're likely to encounter. Note that *Laden*, *Handlung*, and *Geschäft* all mean "store," and most of the time can be used interchangeably.

Table 8.1 Types of Shops and Stores

English	German	Pronunciation
bakery	die Bäckerei	*dee bay-ke-rie*
butcher shop	die Metzgerei	*dee mets-ghe-rie*
candy store	die Süsswaren-handlung	*dee sewss-wah-ren-hahnd-loong*
coffee shop	das Café	*dahs kah-feh*
fish store	das Fischgeschäft	*dahs fish-geh-shaft*
grocery store	der Lebensmittel-laden	*dair lay-bens-mee-teh-lah-den*
ice-cream shop	die Eisdiele	*dee ies-dee-le*
liquor store	die Weinhandlung	*dee vine-hahnd-loong*
pastry shop	die Konditorei	*dee kohn-dee-toh-rie*
pub	die Kneipe	*dee knie-peh*
restaurant	das Restaurant das Gasthaus	*dahs res-tow-rahn dahs gahst-hows*
specialty food store	der Delikatess-laden	*dair deh-lee-kah-tes-lah-den*
supermarket	der Supermarkt	*dair Soo-per-mahrkt*

WELCOME TO GERMANY While We're at It

Although some shops in Germany, Austria, and Switzerland specialize in liquors, beer, and wines, alcoholic beverages also can be purchased in supermarkets.

"I'll Have a Dozen Eggs, Please"

You'll surely find something to buy in the shops and stores you explore. Tables 8.2 and 8.3 will help you tell the clerk what you want.

Table 8.2 Asking for Service

English	German	Pronunciation
May I help you?	Kann ich Ihnen helfen?	*kahn eeH ee-nen hel-fen*
What would you like?	Sie wünschen? Was darf es sein?	*see vewn-shen vahs dahrf ehs sien*
I would like ... please.	Ich möchte ... bitte.	*eeH murkh-teh ... bee-teh*
I would like to have ...	Ich hätte gerne ...	*eeH hat-eh ghehr-neh ...*
How much is ...?	Wieviel kostet ...?	*vee-feel kohs-tet ...*
How much are ...?	Wieviel kosten ...?	*vee-feel kohs-ten ...*

Table 8.3 Containers and Quantities

English	German	Pronunciation
a bag of	eine Tüte	*ie-ne tew-teh*
a bottle of	eine Flasche	*ie-ne flah-sheh*
a box of	eine Schachtel	*ie-ne shahk-tel*
a can of	eine Dose	*ie-ne doh-zeh*
a dozen	ein Dutzend	*ien doot-send*
a jar of	ein Glas	*ien glahs*
a package of	eine Packung	*ie-ne pah-koong*
a piece of	ein Stück	*ien shtewk*

continues

Table 8.3 Containers and Quantities (continued)

English	German	Pronunciation
a pound (456 g) of	ein Pfund (500 g)	*ien pfoont*
two pounds of	ein Kilo (1 kg)	*ien kee-loh*
a quart of (960 ml)	ein Liter (1 l)	*ien lee-ter*
a slice of	eine Scheibe	*ie-ne shie-beh*

Making a Reservation

Table 8.4 lists some phrases you need to know when making a reservation. See Chapter 6 to review numbers, days of the week, and so forth, if you need to.

Table 8.4 Making a Reservation

English	German	Pronunciation
I would like to reserve a table.	Ich möchte einen Tisch reservieren.	*eeH murH-teh ie-nen tish reh-zehr-vee-ren*
for two people	für zwei Personen	*fewr tsvie per-zoh-nen*
on June 3	am dritten Juni	*ahm dree-ten yoo-nee*
at 7 P.M.	um neunzehn Uhr	*oom noyn-tsehn oor*
on the terrace, please	auf der Terrasse, bitte	*owf dair tehr-ah-seh bee-teh*
inside, please	innen, bitte	*inn-ehn bee-teh*

Watch It!

Don't assume the restaurant you'll be visiting accepts credit cards. Some do, but many do not. You'll be safer if you have enough cash to cover the cost of your meal. (See Table 8.17 for how to ask about credit cards.)

Care for a Beverage?

In Germany, as in some other European countries, people typically take a coffee break at about 4 P.M. Coffee houses are popular in Germany, and even more so in Austria—particularly Vienna. And you probably know that Germans also are fond of beer, especially those brewed locally. Table 8.5 gives you words for what will quench your thirst.

Table 8.5   Drinks

English	German	Pronunciation
beer	das Bier	*dahs beer*
champagne	der Champagner	*dair shahm-pahn-yehr*
	der Sekt	*dair zekt*
coffee	der Kaffee	*dair kah-feh*
cola	das Cola	*dahs koh-lah*
juice	der Saft	*dair zahft*
hot chocolate	der Kakao	*dair kah-kow*
milk	die Milch	*dee meelH*

continues

Table 8.5 Drinks (continued)

English	German	Pronunciation
mineral water, carbonated	das Sprudelwasser	*dahs shproo-del-vah-ser*
mineral water, noncarbonated	das stille Wasser	*dahs shtee-leh vah-ser*
soda, citrus flavored	die Limonade	*dee lee-moh-nah-deh*
(hot) tea	der Tee	*dair tay*
wine	der Wein	*dair vine*
red wine	der Rotwein	*dair roht-vine*
white wine	der Weißwein	*dair vies-vine*
blush wine	der Rosé	*dair roh-zay*

While We're at It

> With the exception of bottled water, water typically is not available in German restaurants. You can buy water, but it will not be offered on the menu. And don't expect free refills on beverages, as you sometimes get in American restaurants. You'll be charged for a second cup of coffee or soda in all restaurants.

Foods of Every Sort

Tables 8.6 through 8.16 will help you order foods of every sort.

Table 8.6   Eggs and Egg Dishes

English	German	Pronunciation
fried egg, sunny side up	das Spiegelei	*dahs shpee-ghel-ie*
omelet	das Omelett	*dahs ohm-let*
open ham sandwich with a fried egg on top	der stramme Max	*dair shrah-meh mahks*
pancakes, thin	der Pfannkuchen	*dair pfahn-koo-Hen*
scrambled eggs	das Rührei	*dahs rewr-ie*
soft-boiled egg	das weich gekochte Ei	*dahs vieH geh-kohk-teh ie*

Table 8.7   Fruits

English	German	Pronunciation
apple	der Apfel	*dair ahp-fehl*
apricot	die Aprikose	*dee ahp-ree-koh-zeh*
banana	die Banane	*dee bah-nah-neh*
blueberry	die Heidelbeere	*dee hie-del-bay-reh*
cherry	die Kirsche	*dee keer-sheh*
coconut	die Kokosnuß	*dee koh-koss-noos*
grape	die Traube	*dee trow-beh*
lemon	die Zitrone	*dee tsee-troh-neh*
orange	die Orange	*dee oh-rahng-zhe*
peach	der Pfirsich	*dee pfeer-seeH*
pear	die Birne	*dee beer-neh*
pineapple	die Ananas	*dee ah-nah-nahs*
plum	die Pflaume	*dee pflow-meh*
raisin	die Rosine	*dee roh-zee-neh*
raspberry	die Himbeere	*dee him-bay-reh*

continues

Table 8.7 Fruits (continued)

English	German	Pronunciation
strawberry	die Erdbeere	dee _aired_-bay-reh
tangerine	die Mandarine	dee mahn-dah-_ree_-neh
tomato	die Tomate	dee toh-_mah_-teh
(water)melon	die (Wasser)me-lone	dee (vah-sehr-)may-loh-neh

Table 8.8 Vegetables

English	German	Pronunciation
asparagus	der Spargel	dair _shpahr_-ghel
beans	die Bohnen	dee _bow_-nen
bell pepper	der Paprika	dair _pahp_-ree-kah
broccoli	der Brokkoli	dair broccoli
carrots	die Karotten	dee kah-_rotten_
cabbage	der Kohl	dair kohl
pickled white cabbage	das Sauerkraut	dahs _sow_-ehr-krowt
pickled red cabbage	das Rotkraut	dahs _roht_-krowt
cauliflower	der Blumenkohl	dair _bloo_-men-kohl
	der Karfiol	dair _kahr_-fee-ohl
celery	der Sellerie	dair celery
cucumber	die Gurke	dee _goor_-keh
corn	der Mais	dair mice
eggplant	die Aubergine	dee oh-bayr-_shee_-nah
lettuce	der Salat	dair zah-_laht_
mushroom	der Pilz	dair peelts
	der Champignon	dair _sham_-pin-yong
onion	die Zwiebel	dee _tsvee_-bell

English	German	Pronunciation
peas	die Erbsen	*dee airb-zen*
potato	die Kartoffel	*dee kahr-toh-fel*
	der Erdapfel	*dair aired-ahp-fel*
french-fried potatoes	die Pommes frites	*dee pohm-freets*
mashed potatoes	das Kartoffel-püree	*dahs kahr-toh-fel-pew-ray*
spinach	der Spinat	*dair shpee-naht*

Table 8.9 Pâtés and Sausages

English	German	Pronunciation
black pudding	die Blutwurst	*dee bloot-voorst*
cold cuts	der Aufschnitt	*dair owf-shnit*
fried sausage	die Bratwurst	*dee braht-voorst*
fried sausage with ketchup and curry	die Currywurst	*dee curry-voorst*
goose liver pâté	die Gänseleber-pastete	*dee gehn-zeh-leh-behr-pahs-teh-te*
liver sausage	die Leberwurst	*dee leh-behr-voorst*
sausage	die Wurst	*dee voorst*
veal liver pâté	die Kalbsleber-wurst	*dee kahlbs-leh-ber-voorst*
white sausage	die Weißwurst	*dee vies-voorst*
wiener sausage	das Würstchen	*dahs vewrst-Hen*

While We're at It

Germans are fond of various types of sausages, called *Wurst* and pronounced *voorst.* Cold meats and ham are eaten typically at breakfast and dinner, and warmed sausages, such as *Bratwurst,* are eaten at lunch.

Table 8.10 Poultry, Game, and Meats

English	German	Pronunciation
beef	das Rindfleisch	*dahs reent-fliesh*
Canadian ham	das Kassler	*dahs kahs-lehr*
chicken	das Huhn	*dahs hoon*
	das Hühnchen	*dahs hewn-Hen*
deer	das Reh	*dahs ray*
duck	die Ente	*dee en-teh*
goose	die Gans	*dee gahns*
goulash, Hungarian	das Gulasch	*dahs goo-lahsh*
hare	der Hase	*dair hah-zeh*
lamb	das Lammfleisch	*dahs lahm-fliesh*
pork chop	das Schweinekotelett	*dahs shvie-neh-koht-let*
pot roast	der Schmorbraten	*dair shmohr-brah-ten*
stag	der Hirsch	*dair heersh*
stuffed, rolled beef slices	die Rinderroularden	*dee reen-der-roo-lahr-den*
turkey	der Puter	*dair poo-ter*
	der Truthahn	*dair troot-hahn*
veal	das Kalbfleisch	*dahs kahlp-fliesh*

English	German	Pronunciation
veal cutlet, breaded	das Wiener Schnitzel	*dahs vee-ner shnit-sel*
veal shank	die Kalbshaxe	*dee kahlps-bahk-seh*
venison	das Wild	*dahs vilt*

Table 8.11　Seafood

English	German	Pronunciation
anchovies	die Sardellen	*dee sahr-del-en*
bass	der Goldbarsch	*dair gohlt-bahrsh*
carp	der Karpfen	*dair kahr-pfehn*
codfish	der Kabeljau	*dair kah-bel-yow*
crab	der Krebs	*dair krayps*
eel	der Aal	*dair ahl*
flounder	die Flunder die Scholle	*dee floon-der* *dee shoh-leh*
halibut	der Heilbutt	*dair hiel-boot*
herring	der Hering	*dair heh-ring*
lobster	der Hummer	*der hoo-mer*
mackerel	die Makrele	*dee mah-kreh-leh*
mussel	die Muschel	*dee moo-shel*
oyster	die Auster	*die ows-ter*
pike	der Hecht	*dair hayHt*
salmon	der Lachs	*dair lahks*
sardine	die Sardine	*dee sahr-dee-neh*
shrimp (small)	die Shrimps die Krabben	*dee shrimps* *dee krah-ben*
snail	die Schnecke	*dee shneh-keh*
sole	die Seezunge	*dee seh-tsoong-eh*

continues

Table 8.11 Seafood (continued)

English	German	Pronunciation
squid	der Tintenfisch	*dair tin-ten-fish*
	die Calamari	*die kah-lah-mah-ree*
swordfish	der Schwertfisch	*der shvayrt-fish*
trout	die Forelle	*dee foh-ray-leh*
tuna	der Thunfisch	*der toon-fish*

Table 8.12 Dairy Products

English	German	Pronunciation
butter	die Butter	*dee boo-ter*
cheese	der Käse	*dair kay-zeh*
spreadable white cheese	der Quark	*dair kvahrk*
cream	die Sahne	*dee zah-neh*
whipped cream	die Schlagsahne	*dee shlahg-zah-neh*
	der Schlagobers	*dair shlahg-oh-bers*
yogurt	das Joghurt	*dahs yoh-goort*

Table 8.13 Breads, Grains, and Pastas

English	German	Pronunciation
dumplings	der Knödel	*dee knur-del*
noodles	die Nudeln	*dee noo-deln*
thick egg noodles	die Spätzle	*dee shpayts-leh*
pumpernickel	der Pumpernickel	*dair poom-per-nee-kel*
rice	der Reis	*dair rice*
rolls	die Brötchen	*dahs brurt-Hen*
rye bread	das Roggenbrot	*dahs roh-ghen-broht*

English	German	Pronunciation
sweet or savory filling wrapped in very thin dough	der Strudel	*dair <u>shtroo</u>-del*
white bread	das Weißbrot	*dahs <u>vies</u>-broht*
whole-grain bread	das Vollkornbrot	*dahs <u>fohl</u>-korn-broht*

Table 8.14   Sweets and Treats

English	German	Pronunciation
cake	der Kuchen	*dair <u>koo</u>-Hen*
fancy, frosted cake	die Torte	*dee <u>tohr</u>-teh*
chewing gum	der Kaugummi	*dair <u>kow</u>-goo-mee*
chocolate	die Schokolade	*dee shoh-koh-<u>lah</u>-deh*
chocolates	die Pralinen	*dee prah-<u>lee</u>-nen*
cookie	der Keks	*dair kehks*
	das Plätzchen	*dahs <u>plehts</u>-Hen*
Danish	das Kaffeeteilchen	*dahs kah-<u>feh</u>-tiel-Hen*
doughnut	der Berliner	*dair bayr-<u>lee</u>-ner*
gummy bears	die Gummibären	*dee <u>goo</u>-mee-bay-ren*
hard candy	die Bonbons	*dee <u>bohm</u>-bohngs*
licorice	die Lakritze	*dee lah-<u>krit</u>-seh*
marzipan	das Marzipan	*dahs <u>mahr</u>-tsee-pahn*

Cakes and pastries generally are consumed during the afternoon coffee time and not considered desserts, but Table 8.15 lists some other post-dinner goodies you might want to sample.

Table 8.15   Desserts

English	German	Pronunciation
cold coffee with vanilla ice cream	der Eiskaffee	*dair ice-kah-fay*
ice cream	das Eis die Eiscreme	*dahs ice* *dee ice-krehm*
layers of mascarpone cream and coffee-infused ladyfingers	Tiramisu	*tee-rah-mee-soo*
poached peaches with vanilla ice cream	Birne Helene	*beer-neh heh-leh-neh*
poached pears with vanilla ice cream and chocolate sauce	Pfirsich Melba	*pfeer-seeH mayl-bah*
vanilla ice cream with hot cherry sauce	Eis auf Heisß Eis mit heißen Kirschen	*ice owf hies* *ice mit hie-sen* *keer-shen*
with / without whipped cream	mit / ohne Schlagsahne mit / ohne Schlagobers (Austria)	*mit / oh-neh* *shlahg-zah-neh* *mit / oh-neh* *shlahg-oh-behrs*

Table 8.16 will be useful in case you need a little mustard for your bratwurst.

Table 8.16   Condiments

English	German	Pronunciation
gravy	die Soße	*dee zoh-seh*
honey	der Honig	*dair hoh-neeH*
jam	die Marmelade	*dee mahr-meh-lah-deh*
jelly	das Gelee	*das sheh-leh*

English	German	Pronunciation
ketchup	der Ketchup	*dair ketchup*
mayonnaise	die Mayonnaise	*dee mah-yoh-neh-zeh*
mustard	der Senf	*dair zehnf*
oil	das Öl	*dahs ewl*
pepper	der Pfeffer	*dair pfeh-fer*
salt	das Salz	*dahs zahlts*

Ordering Dinner

In many German restaurants, diners seat themselves. After you're seated, you might have to get your server's attention to get menus and order meals. And remember, Europeans tend to be more leisurely with their meals than Americans do.

Table 8.17   How to Order

English	German	Pronunciation
Waiter / Waitress, please!	Bedienung, bitte!	*beh-dee-noong bee-teh*
The menu, please!	Die Karte, bitte!	*dee kahr-teh bee-teh*
What is today's specialty?	Was ist die Spezialität des Tages?	*vahs ist dee shpeh-tsee-ah-lee-tayt dehs tah-ghes*
What is the house specialty?	Was ist die Spezialität des Hauses?	*vahs ist dee shpeh-tsee-ah-lee-tayt dehs how-zehs*
What do you recommend?	Was können Sie empfehlen?	*vahs kur-nen see ehmp-fay-len*

continues

Table 8.17 How to Order (continued)

English	German	Pronunciation
I would like ...	Ich möchte ...	*eeH murH-teh ...*
I take ...	Ich nehme ...	*eeH nay-meh ...*
Please bring me ...	Bitte bringen Sie mir ...	*bee-teh breen-ghen zee meer ...*
He would like ...	Er möchte ...	*air murH-teh ...*
She takes ...	Sie nimmt ...	*see neemt ...*
Please bring us ...	Bitte bringen Sie uns ...	*bee-teh breen-ghen zee oons ...*
Do you accept credit cards?	Nehmen Sie Kreditkarten?	*nay-men zee kreh-deet-kahr-ten*

Expressing Yourself During Dinner

If you need to ask for a fresh napkin or another glass of wine, you'll find Table 8.18 useful.

Table 8.18 Requesting Service

English	German	Pronunciation
Could we have another ... please?	Könnten wir bitte noch einen/eine/ein ... haben?*	*kurn-ten veer bee-teh nohkh ie-nen/ie-ne/ien ... hah-ben*
Could we please have a fresh ...?	Könnten wir bitte einen frischen ... haben?*	*kurnew-ten veer bee-teh ie-nen free-shen ... hah-ben*
bowl	die Schale	*dee shah-leh*
cup	die Tasse	*dee tah-seh*
dinner plate	der Teller	*dair teller*
fork	die Gabel	*dee gah-bel*
glass	das Glas	*dahs glahs*

English	German	Pronunciation
knife	das Messer	*dahs mes-ser*
menu	die Speisekarte	*dee shpie-zeh-kahr-teh*
napkin	die Serviette	*dee zayr-vee-ye-teh*
place setting	das Gedeck	*dahs geh-deck*
saucer	die Untertasse	*dee oon-ter-tah-seh*
soup dish	der Suppenteller	*dayr zoo-pen-tel-ler*
soup spoon	der Suppenlöffel	*dayr zoo-pen-lew-fel*
tablecloth	die Tischdecke	*dee tish-deck-eh*
teaspoon	der Teelöffel	*dair teh-lew-fel*
wine glass	das Weinglas	*dahs vine-glahs*

Remember that word endings change in German depending on the gender of the word. All words marked *der* are masculine, *die* words are feminine, and *das* words are neuter. Consequently, you'd have to use *einen* here if you desire a masculine (*der*) item, *eine* if it's feminine (*die*), or *ein* if it's neuter (*das*).

Make Mine Medium-Rare, Please

Of course, you want to be sure your steak is grilled to your satisfaction and your vegetables are served with sauce, if that's what you want. Table 8.19 contains phrases to help you along.

Table 8.19 Food Preparation

English	German	Pronunciation
baked	gebacken	geh-_bah_-ken
in batter	im Backteig	eem _bahk_-tiek
braised	geschmort	geh-_shmohrt_
broiled	überbacken	_ew_-ber-bah-ken
boiled	gekocht	geh-_kokht_
browned	geröstet	geh-_rurs_-tet
breaded	paniert	pah-_neert_
not breaded	natur	nah-_toor_
chopped	gehackt	geh-_hahkt_
fried	fritiert	free-_teert_
grilled	gegrillt	geh-_grilt_
mashed	püriert	pew-_reert_
medium-rare	kurz angebraten	koorts ahn-geh-_brah_-ten
roasted	gebraten	geh-_brah_-ten
rare	roh	row
	englisch	_ehng_-lish
steamed	gedämpft	geh-_dehmpft_
well-done	durchgebraten	doorH-geh-_brah_-ten
with sauce	mit Soße	mit _zoh_-seh

 While We're at It _____

> Germans do not typically request sauces and gravies "on the side," as we often do when dining out in America. If you request this, don't be surprised if your waiter or waitress doesn't understand what you want.

Expressing Dietary Restrictions

If you have any special eating concerns, Table 8.20 will help you express them.

Table 8.20   Dietary Restrictions

English	German	Pronunciation
I am on a diet.	Ich mache eine Diät.	eeH _mah_-hke _ie_-ne dee-_ayt_
I am a vegetarian.	Ich bin Vegetarier / Vegetarierin.	eeH bin veh-geh-_tah_-ree-er / veh-geh-_tah_-ree-er-een
I can't eat anything with …	Ich kann nichts mit … essen.	eeH kahn neeHts mit … ebs-en
alcohol	Alkohol	_ahl_-koh-bole
caffeine	Koffein	koh-fay-_een_
dairy products	Milchprodukten	_meelH_-pro-dook-ten
fish	Fisch	fish
gluten	Gluten	_gloo_-ten
meat	Fleisch	fliesh
MSG	Monosodium-glutamat	_moh_-noh-_soh_-dee-oom-_gloo_-tah-maht
nuts	Nüssen	_new_-sen
shellfish	Krustentieren	_kroos_-ten-tee-ren
wheat	Weizen	_vie_-tsen
Does this dish have …?	Hat dieses Gericht …?	baht _dee_-zes geh-_reeHt_ …
Does this drink have …?	Hat dieses Gertränk …?	baht _dee_-zes geh-_trehnk_ …
Could you take out …?	Können Sie … entfernen?	_kur_-nen zee … ant-_fayr_-nen

continues

Table 8.20 Dietary Restrictions (continued)

English	German	Pronunciation
Which dish is ...?	Welches Gericht hat ...?	*vehl*-Hes geh-*reeHt* *haht* ...
low in cholesterol	wenig Cholersterin	*vay*-niH *koh-les-teh-reen*
low in fat	wenig Fett	*vay*-niH fat
low in salt	wenig Salz	*vay*-niH zahlts
low in sugar	wenig Zucker	*vay*-niH *tsoo*-ker
without artificial coloring	keine künstlichen Farbstoffe	*kie*-neh *kewnst*-lee-Hen *fahrb*-shtoh-feh
without preservatives	keine Konservie-rungsstoffe	*kie*-neh *kohn-zer-vee-roongs-shtoh-feh*

Sending It Back

If you have a problem with a dish you've ordered, you can politely ask to have it returned to the kitchen. Table 8.21 will help you with what to say.

Table 8.21 Expressing Complaints

English	German	Pronunciation
Could you please take this back (to the kitchen)?	Könnten Sie das bitte (zur Küche) zurück gehen lassen?	*kurn*-ten zee dahs *bee*-teh (tsoor *kew*-Heh) tsoo-*rewk* *geh*-en *lah*-sen
It is (too) cold.	Es ist (zu) kalt.	ehs ist (tsoo) kahlt
It is too rare.	Es ist nicht durch.	ehs ist neeHt doorH

English	German	Pronunciation
It is overcooked.	Es ist verkocht.	*ehs ist fehr-kohHt*
It is tough.	Es ist zäh.	*ehs ist tsay*
It is burned.	Es ist angebrannt.	*ehs ist ahn-geh-brahnt*
It tastes too salty.	Es schmeckt versalzen.	*ehs shmekt fer-sahl-tsen*
It tastes (too) sweet.	Es schmeckt (zu) süß.	*ehs shmekt (tsoo) sews*
It tastes (too) spicy.	Es schmeckt (zu) scharf.	*ehs shmekt (tsoo) shahrf*

Finishing Up

When you've finished eating and are ready to leave the restaurant, you're likely to have to ask your server for the check, which, with the exception of self-serve restaurants, is always paid at the table.

 While We're at It _____

> Service charges are included in the cost of meals, so there's no need to leave a tip in a German restaurant. Many people, though, round up the check if they were pleased with the service.

Table 8.22 gives you more end-of-the-meal phrases you might need.

Table 8.22 Settling Up

English	German	Pronunciation
The check, please.	Die Rechnung, bitte. Zahlen, bitte.	dee _rayH_-noong _bee_-teh _tsah_-len _bee_-teh
The check is incorrect.	Die Rechnung stimmt nicht.	dee _rayH_-noong shteemt neeHt
We had only (two) …	Wir hatten nur (zwei) …	veer hah-ten noor (tsvie) …
We didn't have …	Wir hatten nicht …	veer _hah_-ten neeHt …
There you are.	Bitte sehr.	_bee_-teh zayr
Keep the change.	Stimmt so.	shteemt zoh

If you choose to, you can spend a great deal of your time in Germany eating, so knowing some of the phrases in this chapter will be extremely helpful. When you've had your fill of sausages and pastries, you can work off some of the calories by going shopping—the topic of Chapter 9.

Chapter 9

I Can't Wait to Go Shopping!

In This Chapter

- Learning different types of shops
- Dealing with shop personnel
- Understanding European clothing sizes
- Using colors and other adjectives

Many people like to shop while they're visiting a foreign country. It's nice to buy something to serve as a reminder of a special spot or occasion, or to bring home gifts for family members and friends.

If you're looking forward to shopping in Germany, you won't be disappointed. You'll find some fine department stores, as well as many specialty and gift shops. So dust off your credit card and get

ready to learn some phrases to see you through
your shopping experiences.

Every Kind of Shop You'd Like

Don't overlook some of the small, privately owned
shops you'll see while visiting German-speaking
countries. The terms in Table 9.1 will help get you
headed to the shops you want to visit.

Table 9.1   Types of Shops and Stores

English	German	Pronunciation
art supplies and paper goods store	die Papierwaren-handlung	dee pah-_peer_-wah-ren-_hahnd_-loong
bookstore	die Buchhandlung	dee _bookh_-hahnd-loong
boutique	die Boutique	dee boo-_teek_
candy store	die Süsswaren-handlung	dee _zurs_-wah-ren-_hahnd_-loong
clothes store	das Bekleidungs-geschäft	dahs beh-_klie_-doongs-geh-shaft
department store	das Kaufhaus	dahs _kowf_-hows
florist	der Blumenladen	dair _bloo_-men-lah-den
jeweler	der Juwelier	dair yoo-vay-_leer_
leather goods store	das Leder(waren)-geschäft	dahs _lay_-dehr-(_wah_-ren)-geh-shaft
music store	das Musikgeschäft	dahs moo-_zeek_-geh-shaft
newsstand	der Kiosk	dair _kee_-ohsk
perfume store	die Parfümerie	dee pahr-few-meh-_ree_
shoe store	das Schuhgeschäft	dahs _shoo_-geh-shaft
souvenir shop	der Souvenir-laden	dair zoo-vay-_neer_-lah-den

English	German	Pronunciation
sporting goods store	das Sportgeschäft	*dahs <u>shport</u>-geh-shaft*
store offering traditional (alpine) clothing	das Trachten- geschäft	*dahs <u>traH</u>-ten- geh-shaft*

While We're at It

Tracht is the word for the traditional clothing that used to be common in the alpine countryside. Women wore *Dirndl* (*deern-del*), and men wore *Lederhosen* (*lay-dehr-hoh-zen*). Although those forms of dress are now reserved for special occasions, you are likely to see women wearing *Trachtenmode* (*Tracht*-inspired fashion) in southern Germany, Austria, and Switzerland.

Dealing With Clerks and Shopkeepers

Upon entering a store, a sales clerk might approach you and ask if he or she could be of service. The clerk might say, "*Kann ich Ihnen helfen?*" (*kahn eeH ee-nen hel-fen*; "Can I help you?") The phrases in Tables 9.2 and 9.3 will help you know how to answer.

While We're at It

Most goods sold in Germany are subject to a 16 percent Value Added Tax (VAT). Tourists can get that tax refunded on items they buy in Germany and take home; however, to apply for a VAT refund, you'll need to get a tax refund form from a stationary shop and have all purchases verified by salespeople. You'll probably need to have your passport with you to have your purchases verified. More detailed instructions about the VAT and how to get a refund will be available with the refund form.

Table 9.2 Conversing About Clothing

English	German	Pronunciation
Can I try it on, please?	Kann ich das bitte anprobieren?	*kahn iH dahs bee-teh ahn-pro-bee-ren*
I wear size ...	Ich trage Größe ...	*eeH trah-gheh gruew-seh ...*
I'm looking for ...	Ich suche ...	*eeH soo-kheh ...*
How much is ...?	Wieviel kostet ...?	*vee-feel kohs-tet ...*
How much are ...?	Wieviel kosten ...?	*vee-feel kohs-ten ...*
I would like to have ...	Ich hätte gerne ...	*eeH hat-eh gayr-neh ...*
No, thank you; I'm just looking.	Nein, danke; ich schaue nur.	*nine dahng-keh eeH sh-how-eh noor*
I (don't) like it.	Es gefällt mir (nicht).	*ehs geh-faylt meer (neeHt)*

English	German	Pronunciation
It (doesn't) look(s) good on me.	Es steht mir (nicht).	*ehs shteht meer (neeHt)*
It's (too) small.	Es ist (zu) klein.	*ehs ist (tsoo) klien*
It's (very) tight.	Es ist (sehr) eng.	*ehs ist (zehr) ayng*
It's (not at all) short.	Es ist (gar nicht) kurz.	*ehs ist (gahr niHt) koorts*
It's (not) long (enough).	Es ist nicht lang (genug).	*ehs ist (niHt) lahng (geh-nook)*
It's (rather) bold.	Es ist (ziemlich) auffällig.	*ehs ist (tseem-liH) ow-fay-liH*
It's big.	Es ist groß.	*ehs ist grohs*
It's large.	Es ist weit.	*ehs ist viet*
Do you have …?	Haben Sie …?	*hah-ben zee …*
Do you have this in (size 14 / white)?	Haben Sie das in (Größe 44 / weiß)?	*hah-ben zee dahs in (grur-seh 44 / vies)*
Where are the changing rooms, please?	Wo sind die Umkleidekabi-nen, bitte?	*voh seent dee oom-klie-deh-ka-bee-nen bee-teh*

While We're at It

> For bargains, look for signs stating *Aus-verkauf* (*ows-fer-kowf*) or *Abverkauf* (*ahb-fer-kowf;* liquidation), *Sonderangebot* (*sohn-der-ahn-geh-boat;* special offer), or *Schlussverkauf* (*shloos-fer-kowf;* end-of-season sale).

If you're shopping for clothes, it's good to know how to ask for what you're looking for. Use Table 9.3 for help.

Table 9.3 Types of Clothing

English	German	Pronunciation
bathing suit (man's)	die Badehose	*dee bah-deh-hoh-zeh*
bathing suit (woman's)	der Badeanzug	*dair bah-deh-ahn-tsook*
bathrobe	der Bademantel	*dair bah-deh-mahn-tel*
belt	der Gürtel	*dair gewr-tl*
blouse	die Bluse	*dee bloo-zeh*
boots	die Stiefel (m.)	*dee shtee-fel*
brassiere	der BH	*dair beh-hah*
coat (sport)	der Blazer	*dair bleh-zer*
dress	das Kleid	*dahs klied*
gloves	die Handschuhe (m.)	*dee hahnd-shoo-eh*
hat	der Hut	*dair hoot*
jacket	die Jacke	*dee yah-keh*
jeans	die Jeans (f. sg.)	*die dsheens*
jogging suit	der Joggingan-zug	*dair dshah-geeng-ahn-tsook*
negligee	das Negligé	*dahs neh-glee-sheh*
overcoat	der Mantel	*dair mahn-tel*
pajamas	der Schlafanzug der Pyjama	*dair shlaf-ahn-tsook dair pee-dshah-mah*
pants	die Hose (f. sg.)	*dee hoh-zeh*
pantyhose (tights)	die Nylon-strümpfe (m.)	*dee nie-lohn-shtrewm-pfeh*
purse	die Handtasche	*dee hahnd-tah-sheh*
raincoat	der Regenmantel	*dair reh-ghen-mahn-tel*
sandals	die Sandalen (f.)	*dee zahn-dah-len*
scarf	der Schal	*dair shahl*
shirt	das Hemd	*dahs hehmt*
slip	der Unterrock	*dair oon-ter-rock*
sneakers	die Turn-schuhe (m.)	*dee toorn-shoo-eh*

English	German	Pronunciation
socks	die Socken (f.)	*dee zoh-ken*
stockings	die Strümpfe (m.)	*dee shtrewm-pfeh*
suit (man's)	der Anzug	*dair ahn-tsook*
suit (woman's)	das Kostüm	*dahs kos-tewm*
tie	der Schlips	*dair shlips*
	die Kravatte	*dee krah-vah-teh*
umbrella	der Schirm	*dair sheerm*
underpants	die Unterhose	*dee oonter-hoh-zeh*
vest	die Weste	*dee ves-teh*

Try This On for Size

If you're looking for a new pair of running shoes and a clerk tells you that you need a size 40, don't be shocked. Sizing of both shoes and clothing is done differently in Europe than in the United States. Table 9.4 offers U.S. and European shoe size comparisons.

Table 9.4 Shoe Sizes

Women's U.S.	Men's U.S.	European
4½		35
5½		36
6½		37
7½		38
8½		39
9½		40
10½		41

continues

Table 9.4 Shoe Sizes (continued)

Women's U.S.	Men's U.S.	European
11½	8	42
12½	9	43
	10	44
	11	45
	12	46
	13	47

U.S. men's and women's clothing sizes also vary from European sizes. Tables 9.5 and 9.6 will help you figure it out.

Table 9.5 Women's Clothing

U.S.	Germany
5 to 5½	36
6 to 6½	37
7 to 7½	38
8	38½
8½	39
9 to 10	40
12	42
14	44

Table 9.6 Men's Clothing

U.S.	Germany
14	36
14½	37

U.S.	Germany
15	38
15½	39
16	40
16½	41

While We're at It

Even with the differences in clothing and shoe sizes in German-speaking countries and the United States, you might still find many clothing items marked S, M, L, or XL. However, a garment marked L in Germany may fit more like an M in America, because the sizing is different.

Watch It!

Germans can be viewed as more fashion-conscious than Americans, so, unless you want to stand out as a tourist, leave your American "downtime clothing" at home. An outfit of shorts, sneakers, a T-shirt, and money belt will brand you a nonlocal immediately.

Does This Dress Come in Yellow?

Now that you have an idea of how to ask about
clothing items, you need to know how to find a
particular item in a style and color you like. Colors,
listed in Table 9.7, will be useful for activities other
than shopping, too.

Table 9.7 Colors

English	German	Pronunciation
black	schwarz	*shvahrts*
(light) blue	(hell)blau	*(hell)blah-oo*
(dark) brown	(dunkel)braun	*(doong-kel)brown*
gray	grau	*grah-oo*
green	grün	*grewn*
gold	gold	*gohlt*
khaki	beige	*behsh*
maroon	weinrot	*vine-roht*
orange	orange	*oh-rahnsh*
pink	rosa	*roh-zah*
purple	lila	*lee-lah*
red	rot	*roht*
silver	silber	*sil-ber*
white	weiß	*viess*
yellow	gelb	*ghailb*

What's This?

To modify a color as light, simply put *hell* in front of it. To modify it as dark, precede the color with *dunkel* (*doong-kel*). So *hellgrün* is "light green," whereas *dunkelrot* means "dark red."

Adjective Endings

The endings on adjectives (including colors) can change, depending on the item you're describing and how that item is used in the sentence.

It is easiest to say ...

> Das ist rosa.
> *dahs ist roh-za*
> That is pink.

Or ...

> Haben Sie das in rot?
> *hah-ben see dahs in roht*
> Do you have that in red?

It's a little trickier when you try to use an adjective to describe a specific item instead of just the general word *das*, meaning "that."

The nominative (nom.) marks the subject or the subjective complement of the sentence, such as in the sample sentence "Who or what is that?" The accusative (acc.) marks the object of the sentence, such as in this sentence, "Who or what do you have?"

Table 9.8 illustrates nominative and accusative forms. For more detailed information on adjective endings, refer to Chapter 15.

Table 9.8 Nominative and Accusative

English	German	Pronunciation
Nominative Masculine Singular:		
That is a red coat.	Das ist ein rot**er** Mantel.	*dahs ist ien roh-ter mahn-tel*
Nominative Feminine Singular:		
That is a red blouse.	Das ist eine rot**e** Bluse.	*dahs ist ie-ne roh-te bloo-ze*
Nominative Neuter Singular:		
That is a red shirt.	Das ist ein rot**es** Hemd.	*dahs ist ien roh-tes hehmd*
Nominative Plural:		
These are red blouses.	Das sind rot**e** Blusen.	*das sint roh-te bloo-zen*
Accusative Masculine Singular:		
Do you have a red coat?	Haben Sie ein**en** rot**en** Mantel?	*hah-ben zee ie-nen roh-ten mahn-tel*
Accusative Feminine Singular:		
Do you have a red blouse?	Haben Sie eine rot**e** Bluse?	*hah-ben zee ie-ne roh-te bloo-ze*
Accusative Neuter Singular:		
Do you have a red shirt?	Haben Sie ein rot**es** Hemd?	*hah-ben zee ien roh-tes hehmd*
Accusative Plural:		
Do you have red shirts?	Haben Sie rot**e** Hemden?	*hah-ben zee roh-te hehm-den*

These types of grammar details can be confusing, but don't worry too much. People will understand what you're saying, even if your grammar isn't perfect.

Stripes, Plaids, and Polka Dots

Patterns describe clothing, so, like colors, they are adjectives and their endings can change slightly, depending on the gender (masculine, feminine, or neuter) and the number (singular or plural) of the item or items they describe. The endings are dependent, too, on the use of the word in a sentence. If you know how to pronounce the pattern type, however, you'll be understood, even if the ending of the word is not quite right. Table 9.9 gives you adjectives you can use when asking about clothing.

Table 9.9 Clothing Adjectives

English	German	Pronunciation
in one color	uni	*ew-nee*
with flowers	geblümt	*geh-blewmt*
with stripes	gestreift	*geh-shtrieft*
with polka dots	gepunktet	*geh-poonk-tet*
in plaid	buntkariert	*boont-kah-reert*
checked	kariert	*kah-reert*

Leather and Lace

Did you ever track down the *perfect* blouse, only to find out it is 100 percent linen and would take you an hour to iron? We all need clothing that fits our lifestyles, so you need to know a little about fabrics when you're shopping. Tables 9.10 and 9.11 will help you know what you're getting.

Table 9.10   Materials

English	German	Pronunciation
cashmere	der Kaschmir	*dair kahsh-meer*
cotton	die Baumwolle	*dee bowm-voh-le*
denim	der Jeansstoff	*dair dsheens-shtohf*
flannel	der Flannell	*dair flah-nel*
lace	die Spitze	*dee shpit-se*
leather	das Leder	*dahs lay-der*
linen	das Leinen	*dahs lie-nen*
man-made fiber	die Kunstfaser	*dee koonst-fah-zer*
silk	die Seide	*die sie-de*
suede	das Wildleder	*dahs vilt-lay-der*
wool	die Wolle	*dee voh-le*

If you want to ask questions about the fabrics of the clothing you're considering, the phrases in Table 9.11 might help.

Table 9.11 Asking About Materials

English	German	Pronunciation
Do you have wool (sweaters)?	Haben Sie Woll(pullover)?	_hah_-ben zee _vohl_(pool-over)
Do you have that in linen?	Haben Sie das aus Leinen?	_hah_-ben zee dahs ows _lie_-nen
Is that genuine leather?	Ist das echtes Leder?	ist dahs _ayH_-tes _lay_-der
What kind of material is that?	Aus welchem Stoff ist das?	ows _vayl_-Hem shtohf ist dahs

 While We're at It

As with clothing sold in the United States, clothing in Germany must be labeled with fabric contents and cleaning instructions. Because so much clothing is manufactured overseas, the labels are often in English. The wool mark and the genuine leather symbol are also used.

If you enjoy shopping in Germany, you'll find lots of it to keep you busy. And after studying the phrases contained in this chapter, you should be able to communicate with shopkeepers and clerks without much trouble at all.

Chapter 10

Asking for Personal Services

In This Chapter

- Requesting service
- Types of personal services you might need
- Explaining your need to shopkeepers

We often take personal services for granted—until we really need them. If you're walking along and a heel on your favorite pair of shoes suddenly snaps off, you'll be very happy to find a shoemaker and be able to ask to have it fixed.

Or suppose you're on business in Germany with a major presentation approaching, and you realize you haven't had your hair trimmed in months. You'll sure be glad to head to the nearest salon and ask for a haircut.

In this chapter, you learn the phrases to request such services.

Asking for Services You Need

Like anyone else, travelers have a variety of personal needs. To locate the particular services you require and then get information about pricing, the length of time required for service, and so forth, you need to know a variety of terms and phrases pertaining to those services. The phrases in Table 10.1 will help you get started.

Table 10.1 Requesting Service

English	German	Pronunciation
At what time do you open (close)?	Um wieviel Uhr öffnen (schließen) Sie?	*oom vee-feel oor* *urf-nen* *(shlee-sen) zee*
What days are you open (closed)?	An welchen Tagen haben Sie offen (geschlossen)?	*ahn vayl-Hen* *tah-ghen hah-ben* *zee oh-fen* *(geh-shloh-sen)*
Can you fix ...?	Können Sie ... reparieren?	*kur-nen zee ...* *reh-pah-ree-ren*
Can you fix it (them) today?	Können Sie es (sie) noch heute reparieren?	*kur-nen zee ehs (zee)* *nohkh hoy-teh* *reh-pah-ree-ren*
Can you fix it (them) temporarily (while I wait)?	Können Sie es (sie) provisorisch reparieren (während ich warte)?	*kur-nen zee ehs (zee)* *pro-vee-zoh-reesh* *reh-pah-ree-ren* *(vay-rent eeH* *vahr-teh)*
When can I pick it (them) up?	Wann kann ich es (sie) abholen?	*vahn kahn eeH* *ehs (zee)* *up-hoh-len*
I need it (them) as soon as possible (at ... o'clock).	Ich brauche es (sie) sobald wie möglich (um ... Uhr).	*eeH brow-Heh* *ehs (zee) zoh-bahlt* *vee mewg-leeH* *(oom ... oor)*

English	German	Pronunciation
May I have a receipt?	Kann ich eine Quittung haben?	*kahn eeH ie-ne kvee-toong hah-ben*
What does it cost?	Wieviel kostet es?	*vee-feel kohs-tet ehs*

Salon Services

Whether you need a simple trim or have decided it's time for highlights, the phrases in Table 10.2 will come in handy at a salon.

Table 10.2   At the Salon

English	German	Pronunciation
I am looking for a hairdresser.	Ich suche einen Frisör.	*eeH soo-Heh ie-nen free-sewr*
Cut my hair, please.	Schneiden Sie mir die Haare, bitte.	*shnie-den zee meer dee hah-reh bee-teh*
Trim my hair, please.	Schneiden Sie mir die Haare bitte etwas nach.	*shnie-den zee meer dee hah-reh bee-teh eht-vahs nahkh*
Washing, cutting, and drying, please.	Waschen, schneiden, föhnen, bitte.	*vah-shen shnie-den few-nen bee-teh*
A coloring, please.	Eine Färbung, bitte.	*ie-ne fayr-boong bee-teh*
a color rinse	eine Tönung	*ie-ne tur-noong*
a manicure	eine Mani- küre	*ie-ne mah-nee-kew-reh*
a pedicure	eine Pediküre	*ie-ne peh-dee-kew-reh*
a permanent	eine Dauerwelle	*ie-ne dow-ehr-veh-leh*

continues

Table 10.2 At the Salon (continued)

English	German	Pronunciation
a shave	eine Rasur	*ie-ne rah-zoor*
a waxing	eine Epila-tion	*ie-ne eh-pee-lah-tsyohn*
highlights	Strähnchen	*shtrayn-Hen*
(no) layers	(keine) Stufen	*(kie-ne) shtoo-fen*
How (long) would you like it?	Wie (lange) möchten Sie es?	*vee (lahn-ghe) murH-ten zee ehs*
that long / short	so lang / kurz	*zoh lahng / koorts*
(even) shorter	(noch) kürzer	*(nohkh) kewr-tser*
medium long	halblang	*hahlp-lahng*
wavy	gewellt	*geh-vehlt*
curly	gelockt	*geh-lohkt*
straight	gerade	*geh-rah-deh*
(no) conditioner, please.	(Keine) Spülung, bitte.	*(kie-ne) shpew-loong bee-teh*
(no) gel	(kein) Gel	*(kien) gayl*
(no) hairspray	(kein) Haarspray	*(kien) hahr-shpray*
(no) mousse	(kein) Schaum	*(kien) sh-owm*
(no) shampoo	(kein) Shampoo	*(kien) shahm-poo*

While We're at It

As generally is the case for services in Germany, it's not necessary to give a tip, although you might want to round up the price.

Dry-Cleaning Services

If you find yourself with a spot on the front of your favorite silk blouse or tie, you'll be happy to know how to request service at the dry-cleaner's shop. The phrases in Table 10.3 will make it easy for you to tell the clerk what you need.

Table 10.3   At the Dry Cleaner's

English	German	Pronunciation
dry cleaner	die Reinigung	*dee rie-nee-goong*
There is a hole.	Da ist ein Loch.	*dah ist ien lokh*
a spot	ein Fleck	*ien flehk*
a tear	ein Riß	*ien rees*
There is a button missing (here).	Ein Knopf fehlt (hier).	*ien knohpf faylt (heer)*
Can you dry clean this?	Können Sie das reinigen?	*kur-nen zee dahs rie-nee-ghen*
Can you mend (repair) this?	Können Sie das vernähen (reparieren)?	*kur-nen zee dahs fer-nay-ehn (reh-pah-ree-ren)*
Can you press (starch) this?	Können Sie das bügeln (stärken)?	*kur-nen zee dahs bew-gheln (shtayr-ken)*

Laundromat Services

It's often advantageous to travel light, but if you'll be traveling for any length of time, that could result in you running short on clean clothing. If that occurs and you're staying in a place that does not offer laundry service, simply head to the nearest Laundromat and get busy. Table 10.4 will help you.

Table 10.4 At the Laundromat

English	German	Pronunciation
Laundromat	der Waschsalon	*dair vahsh-sah-lohn*
I'd like to wash (dry) my clothes.	Ich möchte meine Kleidung waschen (trocknen).	*eeH murH-teh mie-ne klie-doong vah-shen (trohk-nen)*
I'd like to have my clothes washed.	Ich möchte meine Kleidung waschen lassen.	*eeH murH-teh mie-ne klie-doong vah-shen lah-sen*
Is there a free washing machine (dryer)?	Ist eine Waschma-schine (ein Trockner) frei?	*ist ie-ne vash-mah-shee-ne (ien trohk-ner) frie*
Where can I buy laundry detergent?	Wo kann ich Waschpulver kaufen?	*voh kahn eeH vash-pool-ver kow-fen?*
Where can I get coins?	Wo kann ich Kleingeld bekommen?	*voh kahn eeH klien-gehlt beh-koh-men*

Optometrist Services

Anyone who has glasses or contacts knows how annoying and inconvenient it can be when something goes wrong. If you break your glasses or lose a contact, you'll need help from an optometrist. The phrases in Table 10.5 will help you request his or her services.

Table 10.5   At the Optometrist

English	German	Pronunciation
optometrist	der Optiker	*dair ohp-tee-ker*
These glasses are broken.	Diese Brille ist kaputt.	*dee-zeh bree-leh ist kah-poot*
The lens (frame) is broken.	Das Glas (der Rahmen) ist kaputt.	*dahs glahs (dair rah-men) ist kah-poot*
I lost one contact lens.	Ich habe eine Kontaktlinse verloren.	*eeH hah-be ie-ne kohn-tahkt-lin-zeh fer-loh-ren*
Can you tighten the screws?	Können Sie die Schrauben festziehen?	*kur-nen zee dee shrow-ben fehst-tsee-ehn*
Can you replace this contact lens?	Können Sie diese Kontaktlinse ersetzen?	*kur-nen zee dee-zeh kohn-tahkt-lin-zeh air-seh-tsehn*
Do you sell sunglasses?	Verkaufen Sie Sonnenbrillen?	*fer-kow-fen zee zoh-nen-bree-len*

Camera Shop Services

A problem with your camera can be a major issue if you're trying to get good photos as remembrances of your trip or to show to friends and family when you get home. Fortunately, you'll probably be able to find someone to help you if you run into camera trouble. The phrases in Table 10.6 will assist you.

Table 10.6 At the Camera Shop

English	German	Pronunciation
camera shop	das Fotogeschäft	*dahs foh-toh-geh-shaft*
This camera is broken.	Dieser Foto-apparat ist kaputt.	*dee-zer foh-toh-ah-pah-raht ist kah-poot*
This video camera is broken.	Diese Video-kamera ist kaputt.	*dee-zeh vee-day-oh-kah-meh-rah ist kah-poot*
The film doesn't advance.	Der Film steckt fest.	*dair film shtehkt fehst*
This button doesn't work.	Dieser Knopf funktioniert nicht.	*dee-zer knohpf foonk-tsyoh-neert neeHt*
It needs a new battery.	Es braucht eine neue Batterie.	*ehs browHt ie-ne noy-eh bah-teh-ree*
How much will the repair cost?	Wieviel kostet die Reparatur?	*vee-feel kohs-tet dee reh-pah-rah-toor*
Do you sell color (black and white) film?	Verkaufen Sie Buntfilm (schwarz-weiß Film)?	*fer-kow-fen zee boont-film (shvarts-vies film)*

Jeweler Services

The most common need for a jeweler while traveling is to repair a watch that's not working properly. The phrases in Table 10.7 will be useful if you run into a problem with your watch and need to seek the services of a jeweler.

Table 10.7   At the Jeweler's

English	German	Pronunciation
the jeweler	der Juwelier	*dair yoo-vay-<u>leer</u>*
This watch is broken.	Diese Uhr ist kaputt.	*<u>dee</u>-zeh oor ist kah-<u>poot</u>*
The watch is fast (slow).	Die Uhr geht vor (nach).	*dee oor gayt for (nahkh)*
Can you put in a new battery?	Können Sie eine neue Batterie reingeben?	*<u>kur</u>-nen zee <u>ie</u>-ne <u>noy</u>-eh bah-teh-<u>ree</u> <u>rien</u>-geh-ben*
Can you put on a new band?	Können Sie ein neues Armband dranmachen?	*<u>kur</u>-nen zee ien <u>noy</u>-ehs <u>ahrm</u>-band <u>drahn</u>-mah-khen*

Shoemaker Services

Maybe you want to get your shoes shined so you'll look your best for a special dinner or business presentation. Or perhaps you've broken a heel or are having another shoe- or boot-related problem. The phrases in Table 10.8 will assist you in the shoemaker's shop.

Table 10.8   At the Shoemaker's

English	German	Pronunciation
the shoemaker's	der Schuhmacher	*dair <u>shoo</u>-mah-kher*
These shoes (boots) are broken.	Diese Schuhe (Stiefel) sind kaputt.	*<u>dee</u>-zeh <u>shoo</u>-eh (<u>shtee</u>-fel) zihnt kah-<u>poot</u>*
This heel is broken.	Dieser Absatz ist kaputt.	*<u>dee</u>-zer <u>up</u>-sahts ist kah-<u>poot</u>*

continues

Table 10.8 At the Shoemaker's (continued)

English	German	Pronunciation
This sole is worn out.	Die Sohle ist durchgelaufen.	*dee soh-leh ist doorH-gehl-ow-fen*
Do you sell shoelaces?	Verkaufen Sie Schnürsenkel / Schnübänder (pl.)?	*fer-kow-fen zee schnewr-zen-kel / schnoor-bend-er*
I'd like to have my shoes shined.	Ich möchte meine Schuhe poliert haben.	*eeH murH-te mie-ne shoo-eh poh-leert hah-ben*

Knowing how to find and request the services you need will help you navigate confidently in Germany. The next chapter will help you cope in the event of an illness.

Chapter 11

In Sickness and in Health

In This Chapter

- Describing what's wrong
- Knowing body parts
- Understanding the diagnosis
- Discussing your condition
- Supplies and aids

Unfortunately, sickness or injury sometimes finds us, even when we're traveling. Becoming ill or getting injured away from home, particularly in a foreign country, can be extremely upsetting and scary, especially if you have difficulty communicating how you're feeling or what your symptoms are.

In this chapter, you learn how to tell someone how you feel, ask for medicine or any help you might need, and also ask how someone else feels.

Describing Symptoms and Conditions

If you're not feeling well, you need to be able to explain your symptoms to get treatment. Table 11.1 provides key phrases that will enable you to tell a caregiver how you feel.

Table 11.1 Symptoms

English	German	Pronunciation
bruise	die Prellung	*dee pray-loong*
bump	die Beule	*dee boy-leh*
burn	die Verbrennung	*dee fer-bray-noong*
chills with fever	der Schüttelfrost	*dair shew-tel-frost*
constipation	die Verstopfung	*dee fer-shtoh-pfoong*
cough	der Husten	*dair hoo-sten*
cramps	die Krämpfe	*dee kraym-pfeh*
cut	die Schnittwunde	*dee shneet-voon-deh*
diarrhea	der Durchfall	*dair doorH-fahl*
fever	das Fieber	*dahs fee-ber*
fracture	der Bruch	*dair brookh*
gas	die Blähungen (pl.)	*die blay-oong-ghen*
headache	die Kopfschmerzen (pl.)	*dee kopf-shmayr-tsen*
lump	das Knötchen	*dahs knurt-Hen*
pain	die Schmerzen	*dee shmayr-tsen*
rash	der Ausschlag	*dair ows-shlahk*
swelling	die Schwellung	*dee shway-loong*
symptoms	die Symptome	*dee zewmp-toh-meh*
wound	die Wunde	*dee voon-deh*

To express a condition, either yours or that of another person, use the phrases in Table 11.2.

Table 11.2   Conditions

English	German	Pronunciation
I am (He / She is) bleeding.	Ich blute (Er / Sie blutet).	*eeH bloo-teh (air / zee bloo-tet)*
I am (He / She is) dizzy.	Mir (Ihm / Ihr) ist schwindelig.	*meer (eem / eer) ist shveen-day-leeH*
I am (He / She is) nauseous.	Mir (Ihm / Ihr) ist schlecht.	*meer (eem / eer) ist shlayHt*
I am (He / She is) sneezing.	Ich nieße (Er / Sie nießt).	*eeH nee-say (air / zee neest)*
I have an insect bite / sting.	Ich habe einen Insektenbiß / Insektenstich.	*eeH hah-beh ie-nen een-sek-ten-bihs / een-sek-ten-shteeH*
I have a splinter.	Ich habe einen Splitter.	*eeH hah-beh ie-nen shplee-ter*
I feel (He / She feels) weak.	Ich fühle mich (Er / Sie fühlt sich) schwach.	*eeH few-leh meeH (air / zee fewlt seeH) shvahkh*
I (He / She) can't sleep.	Ich (Er / Sie) kann nicht schlafen.	*eeH (air / zee) kahn neeHt shlah-fen*
I (He / She) can't eat.	Ich (Er / Sie) kann nicht essen.	*eeH (air / zee) kahn neeHt ay-sen*
I (He / She) sprained …	Ich habe mir (Er / Sie hat sich) … vertreten.	*eeH hah-beh meer (air / zee haht zeeH) … fer-tray-ten*
I (He / She) fainted.	Ich bin (Er / Sie ist) in Ohnmacht gefallen.	*eeH bin (air / zee ist) in ohn-mahkht geh-fah-len*

How Long Has It Hurt?

When you've told a caregiver what your symptoms or condition are, he or she probably will want to know how long you've not been feeling well. Some handy phrases are listed in Table 11.3.

Table 11.3 Duration of Symptoms

English	German	Pronunciation
Since when (do you have) ...?	Seit wann (haben Sie) ...?	*ziet vahn (hah-ben zee)* ...
How long (are you suffering from) ...?	Wie lange (leiden Sie an) ...?	*vee lahn-ghe (lie-den zee ahn)* ...
Since (yesterday).	Seit (gestern).	*ziet (ghehs-tern)*
For (three) days/hours.	Seit (drei) Tagen / Stunden.	*ziet (drie) tah-ghen / shtoon-den*
It's been a week.	Seit einer Woche.	*ziet ie-ner voh-khe*

Where Does It Hurt?

Being able to describe where you ache or have pain is very useful when talking to a doctor or nurse. And knowing the terms for body parts is likely to come in handy in other situations as well. Table 11.4 lists parts of the body helpful for use at the doctor's.

Table 11.4   Body Parts

English	German	Pronunciation
Where does it hurt?	Wo tut es weh?	*voh toot ehs vay*
My ankle hurts.	Mein Knöchel tut weh.	*mien knur-Hel toot vay*
arm	der Arm	*dair arm*
back	der Rücken	*dair rew-ken*
chest	die Brust	*dee broost*
ear	das Ohr	*dahs ohr*
elbow	der Ellenbogen	*dair ay-len-bow-ghen*
eye(s)	das Auge (die Augen)	*dahs ow-ghe (dee ow-ghen)*
face	das Gesicht	*dahs geh-zeeHt*
finger	der Finger	*dair finger*
foot	der Fuß	*dair foos*
hand	die Hand	*dee hahnt*
head	der Kopf	*dair kohpf*
heart	das Herz	*dahs hayrts*
heel	die Ferse	*dee fayr-zeh*
hip	die Hüfte	*dee hewf-teh*
kidney	die Niere	*dee nee-reh*
knee	das Knie	*dahs k-nee*
leg	das Bein	*dahs bien*
lip	die Lippe	*dee lip-eh*
lung	die Lunge	*dee loon-ghe*
mouth	der Mund	*dair moont*
neck	der Nacken	*dair nah-ken*
nose	die Nase	*dee nah-ze*
shoulder	die Schulter	*dee shool-ter*
stomach	der Magen	*dair mah-ghen*
throat	der Hals	*dair hahls*

continues

Table 11.4 Body Parts (continued)

English	German	Pronunciation
toe(s)	die Zehe(n)	*dee tsay-eh(n)*
tongue	die Zunge	*dee tsoon-ghe*
tooth	der Zahn	*dair tsahn*
wrist	das Handge-lenk	*dahs hahnt-gheh-laynk*

The Diagnosis, Please

To reach a diagnosis, your doctor is likely to have some questions about your medical condition. The phrases in Table 11.5 will be helpful to both you and your physician.

Table 11.5 Talking About Your Medical History

English	German	Pronunciation
Have you had ...?	Hatten Sie ...?	*hah-ten zee ...*
Do you (currently) have ...?	Haben Sie (zur Zeit) ...?	*hah-ben zee (tsoor tsiet) ...*
I have (had) ...	Ich habe ... (gehabt).	*eeH hah-beh ... (geh-habbt)*
There is a (no) family history of ...	... liegt (nicht) in der Familie.	*... leegt (neeHt) in dair fah-meel-yeh*
I am (not) allergic to ...	Ich bin (nicht) allergisch gegen ...	*eeH ben (neeHt) ah-layr-gheesh geh-ghen ...*
I had ... (two) years ago.	Ich hatte ... vor (zwei) Jahren.	*eeH hah-teh ... for (tsvie) yah-ren*

English	German	Pronunciation
I am taking (medication).	Ich nehme (Medizin).	*eeH neh-meh (meh-dee-tseen)*
I am pregnant.	Ich bin schwanger.	*eeH bin shvahn-gher*

Hopefully, whatever is troubling you is minor and can be easily diagnosed and treated. However, as you know, myriad diseases and conditions can occur. Table 11.6 will help you understand your condition and discuss it with a medical practitioner.

Table 11.6   Diseases and Conditions

English	German	Pronunciation
allergic reaction	die allergische Reaktion	*dee ah-layr-ghee-sheh ray-ahk-tsyohn*
allergy	die Allergie	*dee ah-layr-ghee*
angina	die Angina	*dee ahn-ghee-nah*
appendicitis	die Blinddarm- entzündung	*dee bleend-dahrm- aynt-tsewn-doonk*
asthma	das Asthma	*dahs ahst-mah*
athlete's foot	der Fußpilz	*dair foos-peelts*
bronchitis	die Bronchitis	*dee brohn-Hee-tees*
cancer	der Krebs	*dair krayps*
common cold	der Schnupfen die Erkältung	*dair shnoo-pfen dee air-kayl-toong*
diabetes	die Diabetis	*dee dee-ah-bay-tis*
dizziness	die Schwindelge- fühle	*dee shvihn-del-gay- few-leh*
infection	die Entzündung	*dee aynt-tsewn-doong*
flu / influenza	die Grippe	*dee gree-peh*

continues

Table 11.6 Diseases and Conditions (continued)

English	German	Pronunciation
hay fever	der Heuschnupfen	dair _hoy_-shnoo-pfen
heart attack	der Herzinfarkt	dair _hayrts_-een-fahrkt
hepatitis	die Hepatitis	dee heh-pah-_tee_-tees
pneumonia	die Lungenent-zündung	dee _loon_-ghen-aynt-_tsewn_-doong
sunburn	der Sonnenbrand	dair _szoh_-nen-brahnt
stroke	der Schlaganfall	dair _shlahk_-ahn-fahl
tuberculosis	die Tuberkulose	dee _too_-ber-koo-_loh_-zeh

Specialists and Medical Facilities

If you need specialized treatment, you might need to find your way to one of the medical treatment facilities or specialists listed in Table 11.7.

Table 11.7 Medical Treatment Facilities

English	German	Pronunciation
ambulance	der Krankenwa-gen	dair _krahn_-ken-vah-ghen
ambulance with physician	der Notarztwa-gen	dair _noht_-ahrtst-vah-ghen
emergency room	die Notaufnahme	dee _noht_-owf-nah-meh
hospital	das Krankenhaus	dahs _krahn_-ken-house
physician specializing in accident treatment -	der Unfallarzt (m.) die Unfallärztin (f.)	dair _oon_-fahl-artst dee _oon_-fahl-ayrts-tihn
physician's office	die Arztpraxis	dee _ahrtst_-prahk-sihs

Getting the Supplies You Need

When you've been diagnosed and have a recommended treatment, you need to get the necessary medicines and supplies. The pharmacy, or *die Apotheke* (*dee ah-poh-tay-keh*), is likely to be your first stop, and the phrases in Table 11.8 will help you find it and operate smoothly once you're there.

Table 11.8   At the Pharmacy

English	German	Pronunciation
Where is the nearest pharmacy?	Wo ist die nächste Apotheke?	*voh ist dee nayks-teh ah-poh-teh-keh*
I would like to have this prescription filled.	Ich möchte dieses Rezept einlösen.	*eeH murH-teh dee-zehs reh-tsept ien-lur-zen*
Do you have something for (pain)?	Haben Sie etwas gegen (Schmerzen)?	*hah-ben zee eht-vahs geh-ghen (shmayr-tsehn)*
Do you have a smaller / larger package?	Haben Sie eine kleinere / größere Packung?	*hah-ben zee ie-ne klie-neh-reh / grew-say-reh pah-koong*

A store that sells mainly hygiene and beauty products is called a *Drogerie* (*droh-gheh-ree*). Table 11.9 lists drugstore items, or *Drogerieartikel.*

While We're at It _____

Medicine is available only from an *Apotheke,* which normally is marked by a red "A" on the storefront. If the nearest *Apotheke* is closed, look for a sign on the door telling you the location of the nearest all-night pharmacy (*Nachtdienst*) or weekend pharmacy (*Wochenenddienst*).

Table 11.9   Drugstore Items

English	German	Pronunciation
alcohol	der Alkohol	*dair ahl-koh-hohl*
antacid	das Mittel gegen Sodbrennen	*dahs mee-tel geh-ghen zohd-bray-nen*
antihistamine	das Antihis-tamin	*dahs ahn-tee-hees-tah-meen*
antiseptic	das Desinfek-tionsmittel	*dahs dehs-een-fayk-tsyohns-mee-tel*
aspirin	das Aspirin	*dahs ahs-pee-reen*
bandages	die Bandagen	*dee bahn-dah-shen*
Band-Aids	die Pflaster	*dee pflahs-ter*
bobby pins	die Haarspangen	*dee hahr-shpahn-ghen*
baby bottle	das Fläschchen	*dahs flaysh-Hen*
brush	die Bürste	*dee burs-teh*
comb	der Kamm	*dair kahm*
condoms	die Kondome	*dee kohn-doh-meh*
contact lens fluid	die Kontakt-linsen-flüssigkeit	*dee kohn-tahkt-leen-zen-flew-seeH-kiet*
cotton	die Watte	*dee vah-teh*

English	German	Pronunciation
cough drops	die Hustenbon-bons	*dee hoos-ten-bohm-bohns*
cough syrup	der Hustensaft	*dair hoos-ten-sahft*
deodorant	das Deo	*dahs day-oh*
diaper	die Windel	*dee veen-del*
eye drops	die Augentro-pfen	*dee ow-ghen-troh-pfehn*
heating pad	das Wärme-kissen	*dahs vayr-meh-kee-sen*
ice pack	der Kühlakku	*dair kewl-ah-koo*
laxative	das Abführmittel	*dahs up-fewr-mee-tel*
makeup	das Makeup	*dahs makeup*
mouthwash	das Mundwasser	*dahs moont-vah-ser*
nail file	die Nagelfeile	*dee nah-ghel-fie-leh*
nail polish (remover)	der Nagellack (-entferner)	*dair nah-ghel-lak (-aynt-fayr-ner)*
nose drops	die Nasentro-pfen	*dee nah-zen-troh-pfehn*
pacifier	der Schnuller	*dair shnoo-ler*
razor	der Rasierer	*dair rah-zee-rer*
safety pins	die Sicherheits-nadeln	*dee zee-Her-hiets-nah-deln*
sanitary napkins	die Binden	*dee been-den*
shampoo (anti-dandruff)	das (Schuppen-) Shampoo	*dahs (shoo-pen-) shahm-poo*
shaving cream	die Rasiercreme	*dee rah-zeer-kraym*
sleeping pills	die Schlafta-bletten	*dee shlahf-tah-bleh-ten*
soap	die Seife	*dee sie-feh*
suntan lotion	die Sonnencreme	*dee zoh-nen-kraym*
tampon	der Tampon	*dair tahm-pohn*
thermometer	das Thermo-meter	*dahs tayr-moh-may-ter*

continues

Table 11.9   Drugstore Items (continued)

English	German	Pronunciation
tissues	die (Papier-) Taschentücher	*dee (pah-_peer_-) tah-shen-_tew_-Her*
toothbrush	die Zahnbürste	*dee _tsahn_-bewr-steh*
toothpaste	die Zahnpaste	*dee tsahn-pahs-teh*
tweezers	die Pinzette	*dee peen-_tseh_-teh*
vitamins	die Vitamine	*dee vee-tah-_mee_-neh*

Extra Helpers

With the exception of the hearing aid, all the "extra helpers" listed in Table 11.10 can be purchased at a medical supply store, or *Sanitätshaus* (*sah-nee-tayts-house*).

Table 11.10   Orthotics

English	German	Pronunciation
cane	der Stock	*dair shtohk*
crutches	die Krücken	*dee _krew_-ken*
hearing aid	das Hörgerät	*dahs _hur_-gay-rayt*
walker	die Gehhilfe	*dee _geh_-hil-feh*
wheelchair	der Rollstuhl	*dair _rohl_-shtool*

Hopefully, you won't have to use many of the phrases contained in this chapter. As always, however, it's good to be prepared.

12

Ready for Anything

In This Chapter

- Getting and giving help
- Communicating your problem
- Finding the necessary place to get help
- Flat tires and all that jazz
- Addressing a problem or emergency

In the world we live in, we must keep ourselves prepared to deal with emergencies. The more prepared you are, the easier it will be to cope if an incident or accident should occur.

In this chapter, you learn to ask for help and offer help to others, express a variety of situations, and generally communicate with others in the event of an emergency.

Helping and Being Helped

We all need someone to lean on from time to time, and there's no shame in asking for help when you need it. Find out how to get help, and offer it to others, from Table 12.1.

Table 12.1   Asking For and Offering Assistance

English	German	Pronunciation
Help me, please!	Bitte helfen Sie mir!	*bee-teh hayl-fehn zee meer*
I'm lost.	Ich habe mich verirrt.	*eeH hah-beh meeH fayr-eert*
I need an interpreter / a doctor.	Ich brauche einen Dolmetscher / Arzt.	*eeH brow-Heh ie-nen dohl-match-er / ahrtst*
Does anyone here speak English?	Spricht hier jemand English?	*shpreeHt heer yay-mahnt ehng-lish*
Please call ...	Bitte rufen Sie ...	*bee-teh roo-fen zee ...*
the police	die Polizei	*dee poh-lee-tsie*
an ambulance	einen Kranken-wagen	*ie-nen krahn-kehn-vah-ghen*
the firefighters	die Feuerwehr	*dee foy-er-vayr*
I don't understand it / you.	Ich verstehe es / Sie nicht.	*eeH fayr-shteh-eh ehs / zee neeHt*
Excuse me. / Pardon.	Entschuldigung.	*ehnt-shool-dee-goong*
Please repeat.	Bitte wieder-holen Sie.	*bee-teh vee-der-hoh-len zee*

Expressing Your Situation Clearly

When something goes wrong, you need to know how to communicate your situation. The phrases in Table 12.2 will help you do so.

Table 12.2   Explaining Your Situation

English	German	Pronunciation
I lost ...	Ich habe ... verloren.	*eeH _hah_-beh ... fayr-_loh_-ren*
my passport	meinen Paß	*_mie_-nen pahs*
my wallet	mein Portemonnaie	*mien _port_-moh-nay*
Someone has stolen ...	Jemand hat ... gestohlen.	*_yay_-mahnt haht ... geh-_shtoh_-lehn*
my purse	meine Handtasche	*_mie_-ne _hahnd_-tah-sheh*
my suitcase	meinen Koffer	*_mie_-nen _koh_-fer*
my watch / my jewelry	meine Uhr / meinen Schmuck	*_mie_-ne oor / _mie_-nen shmook*
Someone has assaulted me.	Jemand hat mich angegriffen.	*_yay_-mant haht meeH _ahn_-geh-gree-fen*

Getting to Where You Need to Be

In the event of an emergency, you might need to locate a hospital or other facility where you can get help. Table 12.3 provides the names of some places you could get assistance.

While We're at It

> Emergency numbers in Germany are 110 for the police and 112 for firefighters. It's a good idea to keep these numbers handy—just in case.

Table 12.3 Getting to the Right Place

English	German	Pronunciation
Where is ...?	Wo ist ...?	*voh ist ...*
the police station	das Polizeiamt	*dahs poh-lee-<u>tsie</u>-ahmt*
the American Consulate	das amerikanische Konsulat	*dahs ah-may-ree-<u>kah</u>-nee-sheh kohn-soo-<u>laht</u>*
the American Embassy	die amerikanische Botschaft	*die ah-may-ree-<u>kah</u>-nee-sheh <u>boht</u>-shahft*
the nearest hospital	das nächste Krankenhaus	*dahs <u>nayks</u>-teh <u>krahn</u>-ken-house*
the nearest garage	die nächste Werkstatt	*dee <u>nayks</u>-teh <u>vayrk</u>-shtaht*
Is it nearby?	Ist es nahe?	*ist ehs <u>nah</u>-heh*
Is it far?	Ist es weit?	*ist ehs viet*

Dealing With Car Emergencies

Car problems are some of the most common types of emergencies. Depending on the severity of the problem, it can be anything from a nuisance to a tragedy. If you encounter car trouble, let's hope it's something minor such as a flat tire or dead battery. Even if you have more serious problems, however, the phrases in Table 12.4 will help you get the help you need.

While We're at It

In Germany, emergency phones are located along the sides of highways so you can contact highway police if you need help. Tiny arrows on the white posts lining the highway point in the direction of the nearest phone.

Table 12.4   Car Emergencies

English	German	Pronunciation
I have …	Ich habe …	*eeH hah-beh …*
a car accident	einen Autounfall	*ie-nen ow-toh-oon-fahl*
a car breakdown	eine Autopanne	*ie-ne ow-toh-pah-neh*
a flat tire	einen platten Reifen	*ie-nen plah-ten rie-fen*
I need …	Ich brauche …	*eeH brow-khe …*
help	Hilfe	*heel-feh*
an ambulance	einen Kranken-wagen	*ie-nen krahn-ken-vah-ghen*
a mechanic	einen Autome-chaniker	*ie-nen ow-toh-may-Hah-nee-ker*
a tow truck	einen Abschlepp-wagen	*ie-nen up-shlep-vah-ghen*

While We're at It

> If you are in an accident or your car breaks down, you're required to place a red triangle at a sufficient distance from your car to secure the area. All cars are required to be equipped with this warning sign, plus a first-aid kit and spare bulb kit. If you're renting a car, these items should be in the vehicle.

Coping in Emergency Situations

When faced with a problem, it's important to know how to respond to it. The phrases in Table 12.5 will help you address a variety of situations and communicate with others who might be able to help you or might be experiencing an emergency themselves.

Table 12.5 Addressing Problems or Emergencies

English	German	Pronunciation
Calm down!	Beruhigen Sie sich!	*bay-roo-ghen zee zeeH*
Come (quickly)!	Kommen Sie (schnell)!	*koh-men zee (shnayl)*
Don't worry!	Machen Sie sich keine Sorgen!	*mah-khen zee zeeH kie-neh zohr-ghen*
Easy does it!	Vorsichtig!	*for-zeeH-teeH*

English	German	Pronunciation
Fire!	Feuer!	*foy-er*
Go away!	Gehen Sie weg!	*gheh-hen zee vayk*
I have a problem.	Ich habe ein Problem.	*eeH hah-beh ien proh-blaym*
Help!	Hilfe!	*heel-feh*
Hurry up!	Machen Sie schnell!	*mah-khen zee shnayl*
It's none of your business.	Es geht Sie nichts an.	*ehs gheht zee neeHts ahn*
Leave me alone!	Lassen Sie mich in Ruhe!	*lah-sen zee meeH een roo-eh*
Look!	Schauen Sie!	*sh-ow-en zee*
Listen!	Hören Sie!	*hur-en zee*
He (She) is following me.	Er (Sie) folgt mir.	*air (zee) fohlkt meer*
Stop!	Stop! / Halt!	*shtohp / hahlt*
Stop him (her)!	Halten Sie ihn (sie) auf!	*hahl-ten zee een (zee) owf*
Take it easy!	Regen Sie sich nicht auf!	*ray-ghen zee zeeH neeHt owf*
Wait!	Warten Sie!	*vahr-ten zee*
Watch out!	Achtung!	*ahkh-toonk*
What's the matter?	Was ist los?	*vahs ist lohs*

Hopefully, you'll encounter few problems and no emergencies during your travels. It's a good idea, however, to anticipate potential problems and think about how you would deal with them if they were to occur.

Taking Care of Business

In This Chapter

- Getting around at the post office
- Talking on the phone
- Addressing phone problems
- Using computers
- Faxing and copying

If you find yourself in a German-speaking country for business purposes, or even if you're traveling for pleasure, you're likely to need to know some phrases pertaining to phones, computers, and so forth. In this chapter, you learn the phrases you need to get along in the post office, on the phone, and in other business-related situations.

Mail Call

You need to know certain phrases if you want to send or receive mail. Whether you're sending a postcard to friends at home or sending a package special delivery for business purposes, the terms in Table 13.1 will help you.

Table 13.1 Mail and Post Office Terms

English	German	Pronunciation
address	die Adresse	*dee ah-dreh-seh*
addressee	der Empfänger	*dair ehm-pfayng-er*
(by) air mail	(mit) Luftpost (f.)	*(mit) looft-pohst*
envelope	der Umschlag	*dair oom-shlahg*
letter	der Brief	*dair breef*
mailbox	der Briefkasten	*dair breef-kahs-ten*
package	das Paket	*dahs pah-kayt*
postal code	die Postleitzahl	*dee pohst-liet-tsahl*
postcard	die Postkarte	*dee pohst-kahr-teh*
rate	der Tarif	*dair tah-reef*
(as) registered mail	(per) Einschreiben (n.)	*(pehr) ien-shrie-ben*
(by) special delivery	(per) Eilbote	*(pehr) iel-boh-the*
stamp	die Briefmarke	*dee breef-mahr-keh*
How much is (a letter) to …?	Was kostet (ein Brief) nach …?	*vahs kohs-teht (ien breef) nahkh …*
I would like to send this (by air mail).	Ich möchte das (mit Luftpost) schicken.	*eeH murH-teh dahs (mit looft-pohst) shee-ken*
How much does it weigh?	Wieviel wiegt es?	*vee-feel veeght ehs*
When will it arrive?	Wann wird es angkommen?	*vahn veert ehs ahn-koh-men*

Keeping in Touch by Phone

Public phones, most with English menus, are common on German streets and in some cafés or restaurants. Most are operated with a chip card, which you can buy at post offices and newsstands. Table 13.2 will help you know what to do and say at one of these phones.

Table 13.2   Phone Phrases

English	German	Pronunciation
area code	die Vorwahl	*dee fohr-vahl*
chip card for public phones	die Telefonkarte	*dee teh-leh-fohn-kahr-the*
local call	das Nahgespräch	*dahs nah-ghe-shprayH*
(international) long-distance call (to)	das (internatio-nale) Ferngespräch (nach)	*dahs (in-ter-nah-tsyoh-nah-leh) fayrn-ghe-shrayH (nahkh)*
public phone booth	das Telefon-häuschen	*dahs teh-leh-fohn-hoys-Hen*
public phone chip card	die Telefonkarte	*dee teh-leh-fohn-kahr-teh*
(I'd like) to call ...	(Ich möchte) ... anrufen / telefonieren	*(eeH murh-teh) ... ahn-roo-fen / teh-leh-foh-nee-ren*
to dial	wählen	*vay-len*
to hang up (the receiver)	den Hörer auflegen	*dayn hur-er owf-lay-ghen*
to insert the card	die Karte einführen	*dee kahr-teh ien-few-ren*
to leave a message	eine Nachricht hinterlassen	*ie-neh nahH-reeHt hin-ter-lah-sen*

continues

Table 13.2 Phone Phrases (continued)

English	German	Pronunciation
to pick up (the receiver)	den Hörer abheben	*dayn hur-er up-heh-ben*
Do you know the area code (for) …?	Wissen Sie die Vorwahl (nach) …?	*vee-sen zee dee for-vahl (nahkh)* …

While We're at It

Mobile phones are very common in Europe. Don't take your mobile phone from America to Germany and expect it to work, though. Because you'll be in the European network, which is different from what we use in the United States, your American cell phone won't work. If you need a wireless phone, you can rent one at the airport. Or you can buy a Subscriber Information Module (SIM) card that loads credit into your phone when you insert it, allowing you to pay as you go. SIM cards are available at newsstands and gas stations, but they don't work in every cell phone.

"Hello" and "Good-Bye"

Of course, whether you're calling for business or pleasure, you'll want to be sure you have all the phrases handy you might need when you contact someone. Table 13.3 will help.

While We're at It

In Germany, people usually say their last name when they pick up the phone. Sometimes you might also hear *Hier Schmidt* ("here, Schmidt"; *here Schmidt*), or, in businesses, *Schmidt am Apparat* ("Schmidt on the phone"; *Schmidt am ah-pah-raht*). When calling, you should, in turn, identify yourself after your greeting.

Table 13.3   Phone Basics

English	German	Pronunciation
Hello	Hallo	*hah-loh*
Is this the ... residence?	Bin ich bei ...?	*bin eeH bie ...*
This is ... (on the phone).	Hier ist ... (am Apparat).	*heer ist ... (ahm ah-pah-raht)*
Is ... there?	Ist ... da?	*ist ... dah*
One moment, please.	Ein Moment, bitte.	*ien moh-ment bee-teh*
I would like to speak to ...	Ich möchte bitte mit ... sprechen.	*eeH murH-teh bee-teh mit ... shpray-Hen*
He / She is not in.	Er / Sie ist nicht da.	*air / zee ist neeHt dah*
When will he / she be back?	Wann kommt er / sie zurück?	*vahn kohmt air / zee tsoo-rewk*
May I leave a message?	Kann ich eine Nachricht hinterlassen?	*kahn eeH ie-neh nahH-reeHt hin-ter-lah-sen*
I'll call again later.	Ich rufe später noch einmal an.	*eeH roo-feh shpay-ter nohkh ien-mahl ahn*
Good-bye. (on the phone)	Auf Wiederhören.	*owf vee-der-hur-en*

Anticipating Potential Phone Problems

As wonderful as it is to be able to pick up a phone and call someone across town or across the world, we do sometimes encounter problems when using telephones. If that happens to you, the phrases in Table 13.4 will help you handle the problem without losing your cool.

Table 13.4   Problems on the Phone

English	German	Pronunciation
What number are you calling?	Welche Nummer rufen Sie an?	*vayl*-Heh *noo*-mer *roo*-fen zee ahn
I dialed the wrong number.	Ich habe mich verwählt.	eeH *hah*-beh meeH fer-*vaylt*
You dialed the wrong number.	Sie haben sich verwählt.	zee *hah*-ben zeeH fer-*vaylt*
The connection was cut off (is bad).	Die Verbindung ist abgerissen (schlecht).	dee fer-*bin*-doong ist *up*-gheh-ree-sen (shlayHt)
Please redial the number.	Wählen Sie die Nummer noch einmal, bitte.	*vay*-len zee dee *noo*-mer nohkh *ien*-mahl *bee*-teh
This number is not in service.	Kein Anschluß unter dieser Nummer.	kein *ahn*-shloos *oon*-ter *dee*-zer *noo*-mer
Is this the right area code / country code for ...?	Ist das die richtige Vorwahl / Ländervorwahl für ...?	ist dahs dee *reeH*-tee-ghe *for*-vahl / *layn*-der-*for*-vahl fewr ...

Using Computers

If you will be traveling to a German-speaking country on business and will not be bringing your own computer equipment to use, try to find out in advance what equipment will be available for you to use. If you're planning on taking a laptop, ask what kinds of adapters you need and whether they are available. Electrical outlets are shaped differently in Germany, and the standard electrical current is 240 volts. Fortunately, much of the software commonly used in homes and businesses on both sides of the Atlantic is the same. Use the phrases in Table 13.5 for "computer talk."

Table 13.5   Computer Phrases

English	German	Pronunciation
What kind of computer do you have?	Welche Art Computer haben Sie?	*vayl*-Heh art kohm-*pyoo*-ter *hah*-ben zee
Which operating system are you using?	Welches Betriebssystem benutzen Sie?	*vayl*-Hes beh-*treebs*-zews-tehm beh-*noo*-tsen zee
Which programs are you using?	Welche Programme benutzen Sie?	*vayl*-Heh proh-*grah*-meh beh-*noo*-tsen zee
What kind of Internet connection do you have?	Welche Internet Verbindung haben Sie?	*vayl*-Heh *internet* fer-*been*-doong *hah*-ben zee
How / Where can I get access to the Internet?	Wie / Wo kann ich ans Internet?	vee / voh kahn eeH ahns *internet*
Do you have a printer?	Haben Sie einen Drucker?	*hah*-ben zee *ie*-nen *droo*-ker

"Could You Fax That, Please?"

Facsimile, or fax machines, as they're more commonly known, are an important factor in doing business, and they're sometimes handy for personal matters, as well. If you want to send or receive a fax, you'll find the phrases in Table 13.6 to be helpful.

Table 13.6 Fax Talk

English	German	Pronunciation
Do you have a fax machine?	Haben Sie ein Faxgerät?	*hah*-ben zee ien *faks-ghe-rayt*
I'd like to send (receive) a fax.	Ich möchte ein Fax senden (empfangen).	eeH *murH*-teh ien fahks *zen*-den (ehm-*pfahng*-ehn)
May I fax this document (to you)?	Kann ich (Ihnen) dieses Dokument faxen?	kahn eeH (*ee*-nen) *dee*-zes doh-koo-*ment* *fahk*-zen
Fax it to me.	Faxen Sie es mir.	*fahk*-zen zee ehs meer
Did you get my fax?	Haben Sie mein Fax erhalten?	*hah*-ben zee mien fahks air-*hahl*-ten
I got (didn't get) your fax.	Ich habe Ihr Fax (nicht) erhalten.	eeH *hah*-beh eer fahks (neeHt) air-*hahl*-ten
Your fax is illegible.	Ihr Fax ist unlesbar.	eer fahks ist *oon*-lays-bar
Please send it again.	Bitte schicken Sie es noch einmal.	*bee*-teh *shee*-ken zee ehs nohkh *ien*-mahl
Please confirm that you have received my fax.	Bitte Erhalt bestätigen.	*bee*-teh *air*-hahlt beh-*shtay*-tee-ghen

Making Copies

Stores in which you can make copies are common in most parts of Europe, including the German-speaking countries. The German word for photocopying is *fotokopieren* (*foh-toh-koh-pee-ren*), and some phrases to speed you along on your way to making copies are in Table 13.7.

Table 13.7   Photocopying

English	German	Pronunciation
I would like to make a photocopy of this document.	Ich möchte eine Kopie von diesem Dokument machen.	*eeH murH-teh ie-ne koh-pee fohn dee-zem doh-koo-ment mah-khen*
How much does it cost per page?	Wieviel kostet es pro Seite?	*vee-feel kohs-tet ehs pro zie-teh*
Can you enlarge it (by fifty percent)?	Können Sie es (um fünfzig Prozent) vergrößern?	*kur-nen zee ehs (oom fewnf-tseeH proh-tsehnt) er-grur-sehrn*
Can you reduce it (by twenty-five percent)?	Können Sie es (um fünfundzwanzig Prozent) verkleinern?	*kur-nen zee ehs (oom fewnf-oon-tsvahn-tseeH proh-tsehnt) fer-klie-nern*
Can you copy that all on one page (on ... pages)?	Können Sie das alles auf eine Seite (auf ... Seiten) kopieren.	*kurn-nen zee dahs ah-lehs owf ie-neh zie-teh (owf ... zie-ten) koh-pee-ren*
Can you make a color copy?	Können Sie eine Farbkopie machen?	*kur-nen zee ie-neh fahrp-koh-pee mah-khen*

If you're visiting Germany for business purposes, the phrases found in this chapter should be helpful. Remember though, that all work and no play makes for a dull traveler. Be sure to get out and see the sights!

14

Verbs at a Glance

In This Chapter

- Using verbs in the present
- Understanding past tense
- Talking about the future
- Modifying verbs
- Giving commands

A verb is a word that expresses action or existence of something, such as "to sing" or "to be." In German and English, verbs take on different forms. Tenses—past, present, and future—specify when something happens. When we say, "I sing," we refer to the present; "I will sing" refers to the future.

By conjugating a verb, such as "We sing" or "She sings," we indicate who performs the action. We also have a choice of moods: The indicative is a simple question or statement ("She sings?" or "She will sing"), the imperative is a command ("Sing!"), and the subjunctive mood expresses an imagined reality ("She would sing").

In this chapter, we look at verbs and their role in the German language. Let's start in the present.

Here and Now: The Present Tense

The present tense is used to express everything going on now, or in the foreseeable future, such as in these examples:

> Ich mag Rockmusik.
> I like rock music.

> Im Sommer fahre ich nach Zürich.
> In the summer, I am driving to Zürich.

What's This?

German has only one present tense. That means, for instance, that "I am driving" and "I drive" are both "*Ich fahre.*"

Most German verbs are conjugated according to the pattern shown in bold in Table 14.1.

Table 14.1 Regular Present Tense Conjugation

Infinitive	*Kommen*	"To Come"
ich	komme	I come
du	kommst	you come (informal)
er, sie, es	kommt	he / she / it comes
wir	kommen	we come

Infinitive	*Kommen*	"To Come"
ihr	komm**t**	you (all) come
sie	komm**en**	they come
		you come (formal)

Other verbs that follow this pattern are listed in Table 14.2.

Table 14.2   Regular Verbs

German	English
arbeiten*	to work
brauchen	to need
fragen	to ask
gehen	to go
finden*	to find
reisen	to travel
sagen	to say
suchen	to look for
warten*	to wait

These verbs form the du *form on* -est: du arbeitest, du findest, du wartest.

Other high-frequency verbs follow an irregular pattern, as shown in Tables 14.3 through 14.5.

Table 14.3   Present Tense Conjugation of *Haben* ("To Have")

Infinitive	*Haben*	"To Have"
ich	habe	I have
du	hast	you have (informal)
er / sie / es	hat	he / she / it has
wir	haben	we have
ihr	habt	you (all) have
sie	haben	they have you have (formal)

Table 14.4   Present Tense Conjugation of *Sein* ("To Be")

Infinitive	*Sein*	"To Be"
ich	bin	I am
du	bist	you are (informal)
er / sie / es	ist	he / she / it is
wir	sind	we are
ihr	seid	you (all) are
sie	sind	they are you are (formal)

Table 14.5   Present Tense Conjugation of *Mögen* ("To Like")

Infinitive	*Mögen*	"To Like"
ich	mag	I like
du	magst	you like (informal)

Infinitive	*Mögen*	"To Like"
er / sie / es	mag	he / she / it likes
wir	mög**en**	we like
ihr	mög**t**	you (all) like
sie	mög**en**	they like you like (formal)

For polite requests, use the subjunctive form of the verb (as you would in English), as shown in Table 14.6.

Table 14.6 Present Tense Subjunctive Conjugation of *Mögen* ("To Like")

Infinitive	*Mögen*	"To Like"
ich	möcht**e**	I would like
du	möcht**est**	you would like (informal)
er / sie / es	möcht**e**	he / she / it would like
wir	möcht**en**	we would like
ihr	möcht**et**	you (all) would like
sie	möcht**en**	they would like you would like (formal)

The Past Tense—Just Perfect!

In German, as in English, several forms of the past tense exist: the preterit ("I sang"), the present perfect ("I have sung"), and the past perfect ("I had sung").

German uses the perfect tense in the spoken language nearly all the time. It's a pretty safe bet for you to use this tense to relate events that happened in the past. You can see how to form the perfect tense in Table 14.7.

Table 14.7 The Perfect Tense

Subject +	Form of "To Have" OR Form of "To Be" +	Past Participle
Ich	habe	verloren
I	have	lost
Wir	sind	gereist
We	(have)	traveled

Use a form of "to be" for verbs expressing a change of position or condition: *bleiben* ("to stay"), *folgen* ("to follow"), *gehen* ("to go"), *kommen* ("to come"), *reisen* ("to travel"), *sein* ("to be"), and *wandern* ("to hike") are some examples.

What's This?

> To find the stem of a verb, eliminate *-en* from the infinitive form: *komm(en)*, *brauch(en)*, *reis(en)*.

You can form the past participle in several ways. With so-called weak verbs, add *ge-* in front and *-t* or *-et* at the end of the verb stem. With strong verbs, add *ge-* in front and *-en* to the stem of the verb. Strong verbs often change their stem vowels.

Verbs with prefixes like *be-* or *ver-* keep them for the past participle forms. Table 14.8 lists various past participles you might find useful.

Table 14.8 Past Participles

Infinitive	Past Participle	English
ankommen	angekommen*	arrived
besichtigen	besichtigt	visited (for an object)
besuchen	besucht	visited (for a person)
bleiben	geblieben*	stayed
fragen	gefragt	asked
finden	gefunden	found
gehen	gegangen*	went
essen	gegessen	eaten
haben	gehabt	had
hören	gehört	heard
mögen	gemocht	liked
nehmen	genommen	taken
lernen	gelernt	learned
reisen	gereist*	traveled
sehen	gesehen	seen
schlafen	geschlafen	slept
sprechen	gesprochen	spoken
warten	gewartet	waited
sein	gewesen*	been
wissen	gewußt	known
vergessen	vergessen	forgotten
verlieren	verloren	lost
verstehen	verstanden	understood

These verbs form the past tense with sein *as the auxiliary.*

Looking to the Future

Germans often use the present tense to talk about things in the future just by adding words such as *morgen* ("tomorrow") or expressions such as *in zwei Wochen* ("in two weeks"). To emphasize that something is taking place in the future, however, they use the future tense. Table 14.9 shows how to construct the future tense.

Table 14.9   The Future Tense

Subject +	Form of *Werden* +	Infinitive
Ich	werde	ankommen
I	will	arrive
Du	wirst	sehen
You	will	see
Er / Sie / Es	wird	schlafen
He / She / It	will	sleep
Wir	werden	bleiben
We	will	stay
Ihr	werdet	besichtigen
You (all)	will	visit
Sie	werden	nehmen
They / You	will	take
(formal)		

Reflexive Verbs

Certain German verbs must be accompanied by a reflexive pronoun at all times. In English, you can say "I remember," but in German you must say *"Ich erinnere mich,"* or "I remind myself." Some other reflexive verbs include *sich freuen* ("to look forward"), *sich setzen* ("to sit down"), *sich weigern* ("to refuse"), and *sich waschen* ("to wash oneself"). Table 14.10 shows more reflexive pronouns.

Table 14.10   Reflexive Pronouns

Pronoun	Reflexive Verb	Reflexive Pronoun
ich	wasche	mich
du	wäschst	dich
er / sie / es	wäscht	sich
wir	waschen	uns
ihr	wascht	euch
sie	waschen	sich

Modifying Your Speech with Helpers

Modal auxiliaries, or modals, enable you to modify your speech widely in German. It pays to know them, because they occur frequently. Those six modals are given in Table 14.11.

Table 14.11   Modal Auxiliaries

German	English
dürfen	to be allowed to / may
können	to be able to / can
mögen	to like to, to care to
müssen	to have to / must
sollen	to be expected to / shall
wollen	to want to

When using modals, construct your sentences as shown in Table 14.12.

Table 14.12 Constructing Sentences with Modal Auxiliaries

Subject +	Conjugated Form of Modal Auxiliary +	Infinitive
Ich	kann (nicht)	schwimmen
I	can(not)	swim
Wir	müssen	aufstehen
We	must	get up

Tables 14.13 through 14.15 list the present tense conjugations for the three most frequently used modals: *können, müssen,* and *wollen.* (For the conjugation of *mögen,* see Table 14.5.)

Table 14.13 Using *Können* as a Modal Auxiliary

Infinitive	*Können*	"Can" / "To Be Able To"
ich	kann	I can
du	kannst	you can (informal)
er / sie / es	kann	he / she / it can
wir	können	we can
ihr	könnt	you (all) can
sie	können	they can you can (formal)

Table 14.14   Using *Müssen* as a Modal Auxiliary

Infinitive	*Müssen*	"Must" / "To Have To"
ich	muß	I must
du	mußt	you must (informal)
er / sie / es	muß	he / she / it must
wir	müssen	we must
ihr	müßt	you (all) must
sie	müssen	they must you must (formal)

Table 14.15   Using *Wollen* as a Modal Auxiliary

Infinitive	*Wollen*	"To Want To"
ich	will	I want to
du	willst	you want to (informal)
er / sie / es	will	he / she / it wants to
wir	wollen	we want to
ihr	wollt	you (all) want to
sie	wollen	they want to you want to (formal)

"I Command You"

Whenever you order someone to do something, you use the imperative mood. You might say, "Go away!" or "Give me water, please!" or "Excuse me!" Whereas in English there's only one imperative form, German has three. Why? There are separate forms: for commanding one person, for commanding several people, and for commanding in the formal *Sie* form.

For most verbs, the singular is identical to the stem form, and the plural is formed by adding a *-t*. For certain strong verbs, the stem vowel changes in the imperative singular. The *Sie* form, which you are most likely to use, is always constructed simply by the infinitive plus *Sie*. Table 14.16 presents some examples.

Table 14.16 The Imperative Mood

Infinitive	Imperative Singular	Imperative Plural	*Sie* Form
bring**en** (to bring)	bring!	bring**t**!	bringen Sie!
ruf**en** (to call)	ruf!	ruf**t**!	rufen Sie!
komm**en** (to come)	komm!	komm**t**!	kommen Sie!
geb**en** (to give)	gi**b**!	geb**t**!	geben Sie!
hel**fen** (to help)	hi**l**f!	hel**t**!	helfen Sie!

As in any language when you're trying to get a handle on some phrases, verbs are important to assist you with your travels. Some people, however, are a bit overwhelmed by the grammar of a foreign language. Look over the different tenses, and do the best you can.

Chapter 15

Nouns and Adjectives at a Glance

In This Chapter

- All about nouns
- Learning the four cases: nominative, genitive, dative, and accusative
- Understanding declension
- Working with adjectives
- Using personal pronouns

Nouns, as you no doubt know, are things that exist. They are people, places, or things that either exist concretely, as in the form of people or objects, or abstractly, as in the form of ideas. Words such as *dog, door, difference, David,* and *Detroit* all are nouns. They can be replaced by pronouns, such as *he, she, it,* and *they*.

Most nouns have a singular and a plural form, such as *two dogs, two doors, many differences*—maybe even *two Davids*. In German, all nouns also have a gender, and they must occur in one of four cases.

If you're feeling your head starting to spin and you're getting ready to close the book, persevere a bit and read on. This is a grammar reference only, and there is no test scheduled. No one is recommending that you memorize the forms in this chapter, and knowing them by heart won't make you a better speaker. And even if you use the incorrect form of a noun, you'll be understood as long as you chose the right word.

So read on, do your best, and don't sweat it.

Gender of Nouns

German nouns fall into three groups, according to their gender: masculine, feminine, or neuter. Noun gender might seem strange to an English-speaking person because it's not an issue in the English language. You're likely to wonder which masculine characteristics winter (*der Winter*) shares with an apple (*der Äpfel*). And why are both a girl (*das Mädchen*) and a car (*das Auto*) neuter? Table 15.1 will help you to understand.

Table 15.1   Gender in the Singular

	Masculine	Feminine	Neuter
the	**der** Äpfel the apple	**die** Sonne the sun	**das** Auto the car
a / an	**ein** Äpfel an apple	**eine** Sonne a sun	**ein** Auto a car

What you need to understand is that grammatical gender has very little to do with what we commonly think of as gender, and it is rather random. Fortunately, using the wrong gender rarely leads to misunderstandings.

Most nouns found throughout this book are listed with their definite article (*der, die,* or *das*), which helps you figure out the gender. Other nouns have m. (masculine), f. (feminine), or n. (neuter) noted after the word for clarification.

Forming a Plural Noun

As in English, German nouns occur in a singular and in a plural form. Regardless of which gender the word is in the singular form, it always takes on the feminine form in the plural, as shown in Table 15.2.

Table 15.2   Gender in the Plural

	Masculine	Feminine	Neuter
the	**die** Äpfel	**die** Sonnen	**die** Autos
	the apples	the suns	the cars
(a / an)*	Äpfel	Sonnen	Autos
	apples	suns	cars

*In German, as in English, there is no plural for the words a and an. Compare the singular "We eat an apple" to the plural "We eat ___ apples."

There are six ways to form the plural in German, as illustrated in Table 15.3. For many nouns, simply adding -en or -n, as in the English words ox and oxen, will make them plural.

What's This? _____

Again, don't feel that you need to memorize the plural form of every noun you may ever have occasion to use. The correct plural ending is always listed in a dictionary entry.

Table 15.3   Forms of Plural

	Singular	Plural
no ending	der Sommer (the summer)	die Sommer
ending in *en* or *n*	das Bett (the bed)	die Bett**en**
ending in *e*	der Brief (the letter)	die Brief**e**

	Singular	**Plural**
ending in *er*	das Kind (the child)	die Kind**er**
ending in *s*	das Auto (the car)	die Auto**s**
umlaut	der Äpfel (the apple)	die Äpfel

Making a Case

Any German noun occurs in one of four cases: nominative, genitive, dative, or accusative. The case, with its specific ending, indicates how the word is used in a sentence. In English, the order of words accomplishes that:

A large shark bit a swimmer.

Changing the order of the nouns completely changes the meaning of the sentence:

A swimmer bit a large shark.

In German, the word order is more flexible. The endings of nouns, articles, and adjectives determine the meaning of the sentence:

<u>Ein groß**er**</u> Hai biß <u>ein**en**</u> Schwimmer.
<u>Ein**en**</u> Schwimmer biß <u>ein groß**er**</u> Hai.

These two sentences both mean "a large shark bit a swimmer," even though the order of the words is different. To say "A swimmer bit a large shark," the cases (and, therefore, the endings) need to be changed:

> <u>Ein</u> Schwimmer biß <u>einen großen</u> Hai.
>
> <u>Einen großen</u> Hai biß <u>ein</u> Schwimmer.

The Nominative Case

The nominative case shows that a word is the subject of a sentence. In "*Ein großer Hai biß einen Schwimmer,*" *ein großer Hai* is in the nominative. In "*Ein Schwimmer biß einen großer Hai,*" *ein Schwimmer* is in the nominative. The subject, in the nominative case, describes the person or thing acting in the sentence. In the first example, it was the shark who bit; in the second, it was the swimmer.

The Genitive Case

This case is also used in English, even more commonly than in German. It usually expresses possession and is also required after certain *prepositions:*

> the shark**'s** teeth
> die Zähne **des** Hais

Some prepositions requiring the genitive case are listed in Table 15.4.

What's This?

A **preposition** is a word showing the relationship of a noun to another word, such as *into*, *beyond*, or *over*. Think about this sentence: "The arrow flew _____ the wagon." The word you'd use to fill in the blank is the preposition.

Table 15.4   Prepositions Requiring the Genitive Case

German	English
anstatt	instead of
trotz	in spite of
während	during
wegen	because of

The Dative Case

The dative case marks the indirect object of the sentence and is also required after certain prepositions and verbs:

> Bring **me** water. / Bring water **to me**.
> Bringen Sie **mir** Wasser. / Bringen Sie Wasser **zu mir**.

Some verbs requiring the dative case are listed in Table 15.5.

Table 15.5 Verbs Requiring the Dative Case

German Infinitive	English	German Example	English
antworten	to answer	Antworten Sie mir!	Answer me!
danken	to thank	Ich danke Ihnen.	I thank you.
folgen	to follow	Er folgt ihm.	He follows him.
gehören	to belong	Es gehört ihr.	It belongs to her.
helfen	to help	Helfen Sie uns!	Help us!

Table 15.6 lists some prepositions that always require the dative case.

Table 15.6 Prepositions Requiring the Dative Case

German	English
aus	from, out of
außer	outside of, apart from
bei	by, near, at
mit	with
nach	to, for, after, toward
seit	since
von	of, from
zu	to, at

Table 15.7 gives the prepositions that require the dative case when they answer the question "Where?"

Table 15.7   Prepositions Requiring the Dative Case When Answering "Where?"

German	English
an	on, by
auf	on, on top of
hinter	behind
in	in, into
neben	next to
über	over
unter	under
vor	in front of, before
zwischen	between

The Accusative Case

The accusative case marks the direct object of the sentence. It also is required after certain prepositions. In our earlier example, *einen Schwimmer* is in the accusative. In the second example, *einen Hai* is in the accusative. The direct object of the sentence receives the action of the sentence. First the swimmer was bitten, then the shark.

While We're at It _____

> If you're thinking that four cases make things confusing, just be happy you're not studying Finnish. The Finnish language uses 15 cases!

Some prepositions that always require the accusative are listed in Table 15.8.

Table 15.8 Prepositions Requiring the Accusative Case

German	English
durch	through
für	for
gegen	against
ohne	without
um	about, around

Some prepositions requiring the accusative when answering the question "To what place?" are listed in Table 15.9.

Table 15.9 Prepositions Requiring the Accusative Case When Answering "To What Place?"

German	English
an	at, to
auf	on, upon, for, to
hinter	behind
in	in, into
neben	beside
über	above, over, across
unter	under, among
vor	before, in front of
zwischen	between

To help you sort out subject and direct object, picture a bow, arrow, and target. The bow is the subject; action emanates from it. The arrow is the verb. The target is the direct object; it receives the action of the verb.

Declension

You know about cases and the function they fulfill, so now you need to know the actual forms words take on in various cases, as shown in Tables 15.10 through 15.15. The pattern for these forms is called a declension. An overview of this pattern is called a declension table.

Table 15.10 Weak Declension of Nouns (Singular)

	Masculine	Feminine
Nominative	der / ein Student	die / eine Frau
Genitive	des / eines Studenten	der / einer Frau
Dative	dem / einem Studenten	der / einer Frau
Accusative	den / einen Studenten	die / eine Frau

Table 15.11 Weak Declension of Nouns (Plural)

	Masculine	Feminine
Nominative	die Studenten	die Frauen
Genitive	der Studenten	der Frauen
Dative	den Studenten	den Frauen
Accusative	die Studenten	die Frauen

Table 15.12 Strong Declension of Nouns (Singular)

	Masculine	Feminine	Neuter
Nominative	der / ein Äpfel	die / eine Mutter	das / ein Haus
Genitive	des / eines Äpfels	der / einer Mutter	des / eines Hauses
Dative	dem / einem Äpfel	der / einer Mutter	dem / einem Haus
Accusative	den / einen Äpfel	die / eine Mutter	das / ein Haus

Table 15.13 Strong Declension of Nouns (Plural)

	Masculine	Feminine	Neuter
Nominative	die Äpfel	die Mütter	die Häuser
Genitive	der Äpfel	der Mütter	der Häuser
Dative	den Äpfeln	den Müttern	den Häusern
Accusative	die Äpfel	die Mütter	die Häuser

Table 15.14 Mixed Declension of Nouns (Singular)

	Masculine	Neuter
Nominative	der / ein Doktor	das / ein Bett
Genitive	des / eines Doktors	des / eines Bettes
Dative	dem / einem Doktor	dem / einem Bett
Accusative	den / einen Doktor	das / ein Bett

Table 15.15   Mixed Declension of Nouns (Plural)

	Masculine	Neuter
Nominative	die Doktoren	die Betten
Genitive	der Doktoren	der Betten
Dative	den Doktoren	den Betten
Accusative	die Doktoren	die Betten

Adjectives

Adjectives describe nouns and tell how something is: *Green, kind, daring, embellished,* and *informative* can be adjectives. Whenever they precede their noun in German, adjectives have various endings. That is, they match the gender, number, and case of their noun:

> Der *rote, warme* Pulli ist hier.
> The red, warm sweater is here.
>
> Ich möchte einen *roten, warmen* Pulli.
> I would like a red, warm sweater.

When they follow the noun, adjectives do not have endings:

> Der Pulli ist *rot und warm.*
> The sweater is red and warm.

Weak Declension of Adjectives

Depending on whether the adjective and noun are preceded by an *ein* word (see Table 15.16) or by a *der* word (*der* ["the"] or *dieser* ["this"]), the declension is slightly different, as shown in Tables 15.17 through 15.20.

Table 15.16   *Ein* Words

German	English
dein	your, yours (informal)
kein	no, none
sein	his, its
unser	our
mein	my, mine
ihr	her, hers, their, theirs
Ihr	your, yours (formal)
euer	your, yours

Table 15.17   Weak Declension of Adjectives with *Ein* Words (Singular)

	Masculine	Feminine	Neuter
Nominative	ein guter Mann	eine gute Frau	ein gutes Kind
Genitive	eines guten Mannes	einer guten Frau	eines guten Kindes
Dative	einem guten Mann	einer guten Frau	einem guten Kind
Accusative	einen guten Mann	eine gute Frau	ein gutes Kind

Because there's no plural of *ein* (a/an), you must use *kein* (no) to show the form instead, as shown in Table 15.18.

Table 15.18 Weak Declension of Adjectives with *Ein* Words (Plural)

	Masculine	Feminine	Neuter
Nominative	keine guten Männer	keine guten Frauen	keine guten Kinder
Genitive	keiner guten Männer	keiner guten Frauen	keiner guten Kinder
Dative	keinen guten Männern	keinen guten Frauen	keinen guten Kindern
Accusative	keine guten Männer	keine guten Frauen	keine guten Kinder

Table 15.19 Weak Declension of Adjectives with *Der* Words (Singular)

	Masculine	Feminine	Neuter
Nominative	der gute Mann	die gute Frau	das gute Kind
Genitive	des guten Mannes	der guten Frau	des guten Kindes
Dative	dem guten Mann	der guten Frau	dem guten Kind
Accusative	den guten Mann	die gute Frau	das gute Kind

Table 15.20   Weak Declension of Adjectives with *Der* Words (Plural)

	Masculine	Feminine	Neuter
Nominative	die guten Männer	die guten Frauen	die guten Kinder
Genitive	der guten Männer	der guten Frauen	der guten Kinder
Dative	den guten Männern	den guten Frauen	den guten Kindern
Accusative	die guten Männer	die guten Frauen	die guten Kinder

Strong Declension of Adjectives

If the adjective is not preceded by an *ein* or *der* word, the declension is as shown in Tables 15.21 and 15.22.

Table 15.21   Strong Declension (Singular)

	Masculine	Feminine	Neuter
Nominative	guter Mann	gute Frau	gutes Kind
Genitive	guten Mannes	guter Frau	guten Kindes
Dative	gutem Mann	guter Frau	gutem Kind
Accusative	guten Mann	gute Frau	gutes Kind

Table 15.22   Strong Declension (Plural)

	Masculine	Feminine	Neuter
Nominative	gute Männer	gute Frauen	gute Kinder
Genitive	guter Männer	guter Frauen	guter Kinder
Dative	guten Männern	guten Frauen	guten Kindern
Accusative	gute Männer	gute Frauen	gute Kinder

Let's Get Personal

In English and in German, we use pronouns to avoid repeating nouns:

> Shaniqua is surfing the Internet. *She* (Shaniqua) likes *it* (the Internet).

Like other nouns, pronouns have a gender, number, and case in German. Table 15.23 will make it easier for you to sort through the various personal pronouns.

Table 15.23   Personal Pronouns (Singular)

	First Person	Second Person	Masculine	Third Person Feminine	Neuter
Nominative	ich (I)	du (you)	er (he)	sie (she)	es (it)
Genitive	meiner (of me)	deiner	seiner	ihrer	seiner
Dative	mir (to me)	dir	ihm	ihr	ihm
Accusative	mich (me)	dich	ihn	sie	es

Table 15.24 Personal Pronouns (Plural)

	First Person	Second Person	Third Person
Nominative	*wir* (we)	*ihr* (you all)	*sie* (they / you [formal])
Genitive	unser (of us)	euer	ihrer
Dative	uns (to us)	euch	ihnen
Accusative	uns (us)	euch	sie

Grammar in any language can be confusing, there's no getting around it. But don't be discouraged. Do your best and trust that those you're speaking to will be understanding if you make a mistake or two.

Chapter 16

Could We Have Some Order Here, Please?

In This Chapter

- Understanding words and their order
- Placing verbs in sentences
- Putting questions in order

If, at this point, you're shaking your head and wondering why German nouns have so many changing endings, just remember two words: *word order*.

The Order of Words

Word order, also known in grammatical circles as *syntax*, greatly impacts the meaning of a sentence in English. Think back on the example from Chapter 15: "The shark bit the swimmer" versus "The swimmer bit the shark." In German, the sense of the sentence is less dependent on the word order and more dependent on the word endings. There are, however, some rules governing word order in various types of sentences. The normal word order has the verb as the second element in the sentence, after the subject, similar to English, as shown in Table 16.1.

Table 16.1 Normal Word Order

Subject	Verb	Modifier(s)
Ich	komme	aus Amerika.
I	come	from America.
Mein Auto	ist	kaputt.
My car	is	broken.
Ihr Bruder	arbeitet	am Flughafen.
Her brother	works	at the airport.

To emphasize the modifier, put it at the beginning of the sentence. The verb stays in second position, immediately followed by the subject, as shown in Table 16.2.

Table 16.2 Emphasizing Modifiers

Emphasized Modifier	Verb	Subject	Other Modifiers
Am Flughafen	arbeitet	ihr Bruder.	
At the airport	works	her brother.	
Morgen	fliegen	wir	nach Wien.
Tomorrow	fly	we	to Vienna.

If a sentence contains a modal auxiliary, or is in the future or perfect tense, the word order changes just a bit, pushing a part of the verb to the end of the sentence, as seen in Table 16.3.

Table 16.3   Sentences with Modals

Subject	Auxiliary Verb	Modifier	Verb (Infinitive or Participle)
Ich	kann	Deutsch	sprechen.
I	can	German	speak.
Wir	werden	nach Köln	fahren.
We	will	to Cologne	drive.
Meine Frau	hat	jahrelang Deutsch	gelernt.
My wife	has	for years German	learned.

While We're at It

> In *A Tramp Abroad*, Mark Twain claims German word order is quite tricky because it keeps the listener uncertain about what is happening in the sentence until the verb is revealed at the end.

Word Order of Questions

As in English, questions have their own special word order to distinguish them from statements. When asking a question answerable by "yes" or "no," the verb moves into the pole position, as seen in Table 16.4.

Table 16.4 Verbs in the Pole Position

Verb	Subject	Modifier(s)
Sprechen	Sie	Englisch?
Do ... speak	you	English?
Haben	Sie	ein Zimmer?
Do ... have	you	a room?
Ist	das	der Zug nach Köln?
Is	this	the train to Cologne?

Again, if your question involves modals or is in the future or perfect, a part of the verb follows at the very end of the sentence, as seen in Table 16.5.

Table 16.5 Verbs at the End of a Question

Auxiliary Verb	Subject	Modifier	Verb (Infinitive or Participle)
Können	Sie		tanzen?
Can	you		dance?
Werden	Sie	morgen	abfahren?
Will	you	tomorrow	depart?
Haben	Sie	gut	geschlafen?
Have	you	well	slept?

If your question starts with a question word or phrase, such as "Where" or "How long," the verb is again the second element in the sentence, immediately followed by the subject, as shown in Table 16.6.

Table 16.6   Sentences Starting with Question Words

Question Word	Verb	Subject
Woher	kommen	Sie?
From where	do … come	you?
Wo	ist	der Banhof?
Where	is	the train station?
Wie lange	bleiben	Sie?
How long	do … stay	you?

Participles and infinitives will again be at the end of the sentence, as seen in Table 16.7.

Table 16.7   Participles and Infinitives

Question Word	Auxiliary Verb	Subject	Modifier	Verb (Infinitive or Participle)
Wann	wollen	Sie	morgen	aufstehen?
When	do … want	you	tomorrow	to get up?
Um wieviel Uhr	wird	das Konzert		enden?
At what time	will	the concert		end?
Warum	haben	Sie	Spanisch	gelernt?
Why	have	you	Spanish	learned?

Although word order might not seem very exciting, it's significant when you're trying to communicate with someone in German. The information in this chapter is one more step toward speaking effectively.

Chapter 17

Whatever Way You Say It

In This Chapter

- Learning all about idioms
- Understanding rejoinders
- Wishing well—or not
- Remembering what you've learned

If you enjoy words and language, idioms are probably one of the reasons why. Idioms—those words and expressions that enable you to express yourself in a colorful fashion—are the icing on a language cake.

Imagine how dull the English language would be without expressions such as "He's been pretty down in the dumps lately," or "All those questions she asks really rub me the wrong way."

Without idioms, it certainly wouldn't "rain cats and dogs," and you wouldn't be able to "make a mountain out of molehill." No test you took would ever be "a piece of cake," and you wouldn't keep your "nose to the grindstone" to finish a big project.

And just as English has idioms particular to its language, German does as well.

Idiomatic Expressions

Idioms can't be translated word for word—at least not without resulting in some extremely strange translations! The first group of idioms we'll look at are verbal idioms, as shown in Table 17.1.

Table 17.1 Verbal Idioms

English	German	Pronunciation
That's (quite) all right.	Das ist (schon) in Ordnung.	*dahs ist (shohn) in ord-noong*
I don't care (at all).	Das ist mir (ganz) egal.	*dahs ist meer (gahnts) ay-ghahl*
That doesn't matter.	Das macht nichts.	*dahs mahkht neeHts*
There is / there are …	Es gibt …	*ehs geebt …*
It's about …	Es geht um …	*ehs geht oom …*
I'm (not) afraid of …	Ich habe (keine) Angst vor …	*eeH hah-beh (kie-neh) ahnkst for …*
I'm (not) thirsty.	Ich habe (keinen) Durst.	*eeH hah-beh (kie-nen) doorst*
I'm (not) lucky.	Ich habe (kein) Glück.	*eeH hah-beh (kien) glewk*
I'm (not) hungry.	Ich habe (keinen) Hunger.	*eeH hah-beh (kie-nen) hoon-gher*
I (don't) feel like …	Ich habe (keine) Lust zu …	*eeH hah-beh (kie-neh) loost tsoo …*
I'm (not) right.	ich habe (nicht) Recht.	*eeH hah-beh (neeHt) rehkht*

English	German	Pronunciation
I (don't) like ...	Mir gefällt ... (nicht)	*meer gheh-faylt ... (neeHt)*
I'm (not) doing well.	Mir geht es (nicht) gut.	*meer geht ehs (neeHt) goot*
I'm (not) hot.	Mir ist (nicht) heiß.	*meer ist (neeHt) hies*
I'm (not) cold.	Mir ist (nicht) kalt.	*meer ist (neeHt) kahlt*
... does (not) hurt me	Mir tut ... (nicht) weh	*meer toot ... (neeHt) vay*

Rejoicing in Rejoinders

The German language also includes rejoinders, those snappy little comebacks people use to quickly reply to a question or remark. Table 17.2 lists some common rejoinders you might find handy.

Table 17.2   Rejoinders

English	German	Pronunciation
I see!	Ach, so!	*ahkh zoh*
Of course! / It's obvious!	Na, klar!	*nah klahr*
Oh, wonder!	Na, sowas!	*nah zoh-vahs*
Oh, dear!	Oh, jeh!	*oh yay*
Too bad!	Schade!	*shah-deh*
So much the better!	Umso besser!	*oom-zoh bay-ser*
Luckily!	Zum Glück!	*tsoom glewk*

Wishing You Well

Whether you're traveling or are in your own neighborhood, well wishes are always appreciated and appropriate. The well wishes in Table 17.3 will go a long way in creating goodwill, not to mention making friends as you travel.

Table 17.3 Well Wishes

English	German	Pronunciation
Congratulations	Herzlichen Glückwunsch	_hayrts_-lee-Hen _glewk_-voonsh
on your wedding	zu Ihrer Hochzeit	tsoo _ee_-rer _hohkh_-tsiet
on your engagement	zu Ihrer Verlobung	tsoo _ee_-rer fer-_low_-boong
on your promotion	zu Ihrer Beförder-ung	tsoo _ee_-rer beh-_fur_-dair-oong
on the birth of your son / daughter	zur Geburt Ihres Sohnes /Ihrer Tochter	tsoor geh-_boort_ _ee_-res _zoh_-nehs / _ee_-rer _tohkh_-ter
Enjoy your meal!	Guten Appetit!	_goo_-ten ah-pay-_teet_
Get well!	Gute Besserung!	_goo_-teh _beh_-ser-oong
Have a good trip!	Gute Reise!	_goo_-teh _rie_-zeh
Happy birthday!	Alles Gute zum Geburtstag!	_ah_-les _goo_-teh tsoom geh-_boorts_-tahk
Happy (Easter)!	Frohe (Ostern)!	_froh_-eh (u-tern)
Happy New Year!	Alles Gute zum Neuen Jahr	_ah_-les _goo_-teh tsoom _noy_-en yahr
Merry Christmas!	Frohe Weihnachten!	_froh_-eh _vie_-nahkh-ten
With sympathy	Herzliches Beileid	_hayrts_-lee-Hes _by_-liet

What's This?

In English we would congratulate a person *on* his or her promotion, wedding, or birth of a child, but Germans congratulate a person *to* those notable events.

Understanding Insults

Let's face it. Sometimes insults (*Beleidigungen*) are quite a colorful part of language, or at least it seems to be. When you're traveling, especially in a different country, it's always a good idea to be on your best behavior. The insults in Table 17.4, then, are intended more for your amusement and information than for actual use.

Table 17.4   Insults

English	German	Pronunciation
the silly goose	die alberne Gans	*dee <u>ahl</u>-bayr-neh gahns*
the jerk (the candelabra)	der Armleuchter	*dair <u>ahrm</u>-loyH-ter*
the know-it-all (the better-knower)	der / die Besser-wisser (-in)	*dair / dee <u>beh</u>-ser-<u>vee</u>-ser (in)*
the lazy bum (the layer of mold)	der Faulpelz	*dair <u>fowl</u>-pehlts*
the mean guy	der Fiesling	*dair <u>fees</u>-leeng*

continues

Table 17.4 Insults (continued)

English	German	Pronunciation
the dummy (the wood head)	der Holzkopf	*dair hohlts-kohpf*
the jerk	der Schuft	*dair shooft*
the smartie-pants	der Schlaumeier	*dair shlow-mie-er*
the softie (the soft-boiled egg)	das Weichei	*dahs veiH-ie*
the dysfunctional genius (the distracted professor)	der zerstreute Professor	*dair tser-shtroy-teh proh-feh-sohr*
the coward	der Feigling	*dair fie-gleeng*

How Cool Is That—or Not?

Just as in English, *cool* is a hot word in German. In fact, there are at least eight ways to say *cool* in German and at least six ways to express that something is, indeed, "not cool," as shown in Tables 17.5 and 17.6.

Table 17.5 Ways to Say "Cool"

German	Pronunciation
affengeil*	*ah-fen-giel*
cool*	*cool*
geil*	*giel*
heiß	*hies*
stark	*shtahrk*

German	Pronunciation
super	*zoo-per*
toll	*tohl*
prima	*pree-ma*

Watch It!

The asterisked (*) words in Tables 17.5 and 17.6 belong more to the youth language. Travelers over age 40 or so might want to think twice before using those variations of *cool* or *uncool*.

Table 17.6   Ways to Say "Not Cool"

German	Pronunciation
ätzend*	*eh-tsehnt*
bescheuert	*beh-shoy-ert*
doof	*dohf*
furchtbar	*foorHt-bar*
lahm	*lahm*
zum Kotzen*	*tsoom koh-tsen*

Getting Colorful

The expressions in Table 17.7 are more suited to advanced learners than beginners, but you might enjoy having a look at them and trying out the pronunciations.

Table 17.7 Colorful Expressions

English	German	Pronunciation
to be clumsy (to have two left thumbs)	zwei linke Daumen haben	*tsvie leen-keh dow-men hah-ben*
to have your cake and eat it (to dance at two weddings)	auf zwei Hochzeiten tanzen	*owf tsvie hohkh-tsie-ten tahn-tsehn*
to commit a faux pas (to step into the grease pot)	ins Fettnäpfchen treten	*eens fat-naypf-Hen tray-ten*
to be between two conflicting parties (to sit between two chairs)	zwischen zwei Stühlen sitzen	*tsvee-shen tsvie shtew-len zee-tsen*
to not get the big picture (to not see the forest for the trees)	den Wald vor Bäumen nicht sehen	*dayn vahlt for boy-men neeHt zeh-ehn*
to know it all / to be clever (to eat wisdom by the spoonfuls)	die Weisheit mit Löffeln essen	*dee vies-hiet meet lur-feln eh-sen*
to pull teeth (to pull worms from someone's nose)	jemandem die Würmer aus der Nase ziehen	*yeh-man-dehm dee vewr-mer ows dair nah-zeh tsee-ehn*

Now That You've Got It, Don't Lose It!

If you've worked through this book, chances are you know a lot more about the German language than you did when you first picked it up. No, you're not an expert—not by a long shot. But you should be fairly comfortable with the pronunciation of most words and have a pretty good handle on common words and phrases.

So how are you going to be sure you don't lose your newfound German skills? You practice! Keep this book handy, and look through it often, reviewing a couple tables at a time. And if you have the opportunity to converse with a German-speaking person, be sure you do so. Listening is still the best way to learn a language.

Glossary

English to German

English	German	Pronunciation
accident	Unfall (m.)	_oon_-fahl
afternoon	Nachmittag (m.)	_nakh_-mee-tahk
airport	Flughafen (m.)	_flook_-hah-fen
autumn	Herbst (m.)	hairpst
baby	Baby (n.)	_beh_-bee
baggage claim	Gepäckausgabe (f.)	geh-_pak_-ows-gah-beh
bakery	Bäckerei (f.)	_bay_-keh-rie
beach	Strand (m.)	shtrahnt
bird	Vogel (m.)	_foh_-ghel
black	schwarz	shvahrts
blue	blau	_blah_-oo
bookstore	Buchhandlung (f.)	_booH_-hahnd-loong
boy	Junge (m.)	_yoong_-eh
bread	Brot (n.)	broht
brother	Bruder (m.)	_broo_-der
brown	braun	brown
bus stop	Bushaltestelle (f.)	_boos_-hahl-teh-steh-leh
camera	Fotoapparat (m.)	_foh_-toh-ah-pah-raht
candy	Süssigkeiten (f. pl.)	_zew_-seeH-kie-ten
car	Auto (n.)	_ow_-toh
cat	Katze (f.)	_kah_-tse
cell phone	Handy (n.)	_hen_-dee
child	Kind (n.)	keent
church	Kirche (f.)	_keer_-Heh
coat	Mantel (m.)	_mahn_-tel

continues

continued

English	German	Pronunciation
coffee	Kaffee (m.)	kah-*fay*
cold	kalt	*kahlt*
concert	Konzert (n.)	*kohn*-tsert
credit card	Kreditkarte (f.)	kreh-*deet*-kahr-teh
department store	Kaufhaus (n.)	*kowf*-hows
dog	Hund (m.)	*hoont*
drink	Getränk (n.)	ghe-*traynk*
drug store	Drogerie (f.)	droh-ghe-*ree*
early	früh	*frew*
embassy	Botschaft (f.)	*boht*-shahft
evening	Abend (m.)	*ah*-bent
far	weit	*viet*
father	Vater (m.)	*fah*-ter
(to) find	finden	*fin*-den
Friday	Freitag (m.)	*frie*-tahk
friend	Freund (m.)	*froynt*
	Freundin (f.)	*froyn*-din
fruit	Obst (n.)	*ohpst*
gas station	Tankstelle (f.)	*tahnk*-shteh-leh
girl	Mädchen (n.)	*mayd*-Hen
good-bye	Auf Wiedersehen	owf *vee*-der-seh-ehn
green	grün	*grewn*
grocery store	Lebensmittel-laden (m.)	*leh*-bens-mee-tel-lah-den
hamburger	Hamburger (m.)	*hahm*-boor-gher
hello	Hallo	hah-*loh*
help	Hilfe (f.)	*hill*-feh
hot	heiß	*hies*

English	German	Pronunciation
hotel	Hotel (n.)	*hoh-tel*
house	Haus (n.)	*hows*
hungry	hungrig	*hoong-reeH*
husband	Ehemann (m.)	*ay-eh-mahn*
immediately	sofort	*zoh-fort*
information	Auskunft (f.)	*ows-koonft*
	Information (f.)	*een-for-mah-tsyohn*
large	groß	*grohs*
late	spät	*shpayt*
(to) lose	verlieren	*fer-lee-ren*
man	Mann (m.)	*mahn*
meat	Fleisch (n.)	*flaysh*
Monday	Montag (m.)	*mohn-tahk*
money	Geld (n.)	*ghelt*
money exchange	Geldwechsel (m.)	*ghelt-vayk-sel*
morning	Morgen (m.)	*mohr-ghen*
mother	Mutter (f.)	*moo-ter*
museum	Museum (n.)	*moo-zay-oom*
near	nahe	*nah-eh*
(I) need	(ich) brauche	*(eeH) brow-He*
newspaper	Zeitung (f.)	*tsie-toong*
night	Nacht (f.)	*nahkht*
nightclub	Bar (f.)	*bahr*
no	nein	*nine*
nothing	nichts	*neeHts*

continues

continued

English	German	Pronunciation
orange	orange	*oh-rahnsh*
paper	Papier (n.)	*pah-peer*
parents	Eltern (pl.)	*ehl-tern*
passport	Paß	*pahs*
please	bitte	*bee-teh*
pocketbook	Handtasche (f.)	*hahn-tah-sheh*
police	Polizei (f.)	*poh-lee-tsie*
problem	Problem (n.)	*proh-blehm*
rain	Regen (m.)	*reh-ghen*
red	rot	*roht*
rental car	Mietwagen (m.)	*meet-vah-ghen*
	Leihwagen (m.)	*lie-vah-gehen*
reservation	Reservierung (f.)	*reh-zer-vee-roong*
rest room	Toilette (f.)	*toy-leh-teh*
restaurant	Restaurant (n.)	*res-toh-rahn*
Saturday	Samstag (m.)	*zahms-tahk*
sick	krank	*krahnk*
sister	Schwester (f.)	*shvehs-ter*
small	klein	*klien*
snow	Schnee (m.)	*shnay*
soda	Limonade (f.)	*lee-moh-nah-deh*
spring	Früling (m.)	*frew-leeng*
subway	U-Bahn (f.)	*oo-bahn*
summer	Sommer (m.)	*zoh-mer*
sun	Sonne (f.)	*zoh-ne*
Sunday	Sonntag (m.)	*zon-tahk*
sunscreen	Sonnencreme (f.)	*zoh-nen-kraym*
sweater	Pullover (m.)	*pull-oh-ver*

English	German	Pronunciation
taxi	Taxi (n.)	*taxi*
tea	Tee (m.)	*tay*
telephone	Telefon (n.)	*teh-leh-fohn*
thank you	Danke	*dahng-keh*
Thursday	Donnerstag (m.)	*doh-ners-tahk*
tired	müde	*mew-deh*
tomorrow	morgen	*mor-ghen*
train	Zug (m.)	*tsook*
train station	Bahnhof (m.)	*bahn-hohf*
Tuesday	Dienstag (m.)	*deens-tahk*
umbrella	Regenschirm (m.)	*reh-ghen-sheerm*
wallet	Portemonnaie (n.)	*port-moh-nay*
Wednesday	Mittwoch (m.)	*mit-vohkh*
white	weiß	*vies*
wife	Ehefrau (f.)	*ay-eh-frow*
windy	windig	*vin-deeH*
winter	Winter (m.)	*vin-ter*
woman	Frau (f.)	*frow*
yellow	gelb	*gehlp*
yes	ja	*yah*
yesterday	gestern	*ghehs-tern*

German to English

German	Pronunciation	English
Abend (m.)	*ah-bent*	evening
Auf Wiedersehen	*owf vee-der-seh-ehn*	good-bye

continues

continued

German	Pronunciation	English
Auskunft (f.)	*ows-koonft*	information
Auto (n.)	*ow-toh*	car
Baby (n.)	*beh-bee*	baby
Bäckerei (f.)	*bay-keh-rie*	bakery
Bahnhof (m.)	*bahn-hohf*	train station
Bar (f.)	*bahr*	nightclub
bitte	*bee-teh*	please
blau	*blah-oo*	blue
Botschaft (f.)	*boht-shahft*	embassy
(ich) brauche	*(eeH) brow-He*	(I) need
braun	*brown*	brown
Brot (n.)	*broht*	bread
Bruder (m.)	*broo-der*	brother
Buchhandlung (f.)	*booH-hahnd-loong*	bookstore
Bushaltestelle (f.)	*boos-hahl-teh-steh-leh*	bus stop
Danke	*dahng-keh*	thank you
Dienstag (m.)	*deens-tahk*	Tuesday
Donnerstag (m.)	*doh-ners-tahk*	Thursday
Drogerie (f.)	*droh-ghe-ree*	drug store
Ehefrau (f.)	*ay-eh-frow*	wife
Ehemann (m.)	*ay-eh-mahn*	husband
Eltern, pl.	*ehl-tern*	parents
finden	*fin-den*	(to) find
Fleisch (n.)	*flaysh*	meat
Flughafen (m.)	*flook-hah-fen*	airport
Fotoapparat (m.)	*foh-toh-ah-pah-raht*	camera

German	Pronunciation	English
Frau (f.)	*frow*	woman
Freitag (m.)	*frie-tahk*	Friday
Freund (m.)	*froynt*	friend (male)
Freundin (f.)	*froyn-din*	friend (female)
früh	*frew*	early
Früling (m.)	*frew-leeng*	spring
gelb	*gehlp*	yellow
Geld (n.)	*ghelt*	money
Geldwechsel (m.)	*ghelt-vayk-sel*	money exchange
Gepäckausgabe (f.)	*geh-pak-ows-gah-beh*	baggage claim
gestern	*ghehs-tern*	yesterday
Getränk (n.)	*ghe-traynk*	drink
groß	*grohs*	large
grün	*grewn*	green
Hallo	*hah-loh*	hello
Hamburger (m.)	*hahm-boor-gher*	hamburger
Handtasche (f.)	*hahn-tah-sheh*	pocketbook
Handy (n.)	*hen-dee*	cell phone
Haus (n.)	*hows*	house
heiß	*hies*	hot
Herbst (m.)	*hairpst*	autumn
Hilfe (f.)	*hill-feh*	help
Hotel (n.)	*hoh-tel*	hotel
Hund (m.)	*hoont*	dog
hungrig	*hoong-reeH*	hungry
Information (f.)	*een-for-mah-tsyohn*	information

continues

continued

German	Pronunciation	English
ja	*yah*	yes
Junge (m.)	*yoong-eh*	boy
Kaffee (m.)	*kah-fay*	coffee
kalt	*kahlt*	cold
Katze (f.)	*kah-tse*	cat
Kaufhaus (n.)	*kowf-hows*	department store
Kind (n.)	*keent*	child
Kirche (f.)	*keer-Heh*	church
klein	*klien*	small
Konzert (n.)	*kohn-tsert*	concert
krank	*krahnk*	sick
Kreditkarte (f.)	*kreh-deet-kahr-teh*	credit card
Lebensmittelladen (m.)	*leh-bens-mee-tel-lah-den*	grocery store
Leihwagen (m.)	*lie-vah-ghen*	rental car
Limonade (f.)	*lee-moh-nah-deh*	soda
Mädchen (n.)	*mayd-Hen*	girl
Mann (m.)	*mahn*	man
Mantel (m.)	*mahn-tel*	coat
Mietwagen (m.)	*meet-vah-ghen*	rental car
Mittwoch (m.)	*mit-vohkh*	Wednesday
Montag (m.)	*mohn-tahk*	Monday
morgen	*mor-ghen*	tomorrow
Morgen (m.)	*mohr-ghen*	morning
müde	*mew-deh*	tired
Museum (n.)	*moo-zay-oom*	museum
Mutter (f.)	*moo-ter*	mother

German	Pronunciation	English
Nachmittag (m.)	_nakh-mee-tahk_	afternoon
Nacht (f.)	_nahkht_	night
nahe	_nah-eh_	near
nein	_nine_	no
nichts	_neeHts_	nothing
Obst (n.)	_ohpst_	fruit
orange	_oh-rahnsh_	orange
Paß (m.)	_pahs_	passport
Papier (n.)	_pah-peer_	paper
Polizei (f.)	_poh-lee-tsie_	police
Portemonnaie (n.)	_port-moh-nay_	wallet
Problem (n.)	_proh-blehm_	problem
Pullover (m.)	_pull-oh-ver_	sweater
Regen (m.)	_reh-ghen_	rain
Regenschirm (m.)	_reh-ghen-sheerm_	umbrella
Reservierung (f.)	_reh-zer-vee-roong_	reservation
Restaurant (n.)	_res-toh-rahn_	restaurant
rot	_roht_	red
Samstag (m.)	_zahms-tahk_	Saturday
Schnee (m.)	_shnay_	snow
schwarz	_shvahrts_	black
Schwester (f.)	_shvehs-ter_	sister
sofort	_zoh-fort_	immediately
Sommer (m.)	_zoh-mer_	summer
Sonne (f.)	_zoh-ne_	sun
Sonnencreme (f.)	_zoh-nen-kraym_	sunscreen
Sonntag (m.)	_zon-tahk_	Sunday

continues

continued

German	Pronunciation	English
spät	*shpayt*	late
Strand (m.)	*shtrahnt*	beach
Süssigkeiten (f. pl.)	*zew-seeH-kie-ten*	candy
Tankstelle (f.)	*tahnk-shteh-leh*	gas station
Taxi (n.)	*taxi*	taxi
Tee (m.)	*tay*	tea
Telefon (n.)	*teh-leh-fohn*	telephone
Toilette (f.)	*toy-leh-teh*	rest room
U-Bahn (f.)	*oo-hahn*	subway
Unfall (m.)	*oon-fahl*	accident
Vater (m.)	*fah-ter*	father
verlieren	*fer-lee-ren*	(to) lose
Vogel (m.)	*foh-ghel*	bird
weiß	*vies*	white
weit	*viet*	far
windig	*vin-deeH*	windy
Winter (m.)	*vin-ter*	winter
Zeitung (f.)	*tsie-toong*	newspaper
Zug (m.)	*tsook*	train

Index

V

W-X-Y-Z

About the Authors

Angelika Körner grew up in Germany's idyllic Nahe Valley. From her Viennese mother she not only learned standard German, but she also picked up the Viennese dialect. Since moving to the United States, Körner has been teaching foreign language and is currently in her ninth year, teaching in a private school in Lancaster, Pennsylvania.

She frequently visits her family and friends in Germany. Körner lives near Lancaster, Pennsylvania, with her husband, son, and trilingual parrot.

Susan Shelly is a freelance writer and researcher. A former newspaper reporter and columnist, she has written freelance material for an online news service and for various magazines, newspapers, businesses, and agencies. Her other works have included corporate histories, guides to networking and business research, health- and family-related publications, *The Complete Idiot's Guide to Learning Sign Language*, and *The Complete Idiot's Guide to Science Fair Projects*. Shelly lives with her husband and two children in Shillington, Pennsylvania.